Handwritten Recipes

MICHAEL POPEK

Handwritten Recipes

A Bookseller's Collection of Curious and Wonderful Recipes Forgotten Between the Pages

A PERIGEE BOOK

A PERIGEE BOOK
Published by the Penguin Group
Penguin Group (USA) Inc.
375 Hudson Street, New York, New York 10014, USA

Penguin Group (Canada), 90 Eglinton Avenue East, Suite 700, Toronto, Ontario M4P 2Y3, Canada
(a division of Pearson Penguin Canada Inc.) • Penguin Books Ltd., 80 Strand, London WC2R 0RL,
England • Penguin Group Ireland, 25 St. Stephen's Green, Dublin 2, Ireland (a division of Penguin
Books Ltd.) • Penguin Group (Australia), 250 Camberwell Road, Camberwell, Victoria 3124,
Australia (a division of Pearson Australia Group Pty. Ltd.) • Penguin Books India Pvt. Ltd., 11
Community Centre, Panchsheel Park, New Delhi—110 017, India • Penguin Group (NZ), 67
Apollo Drive, Rosedale, Auckland 0632, New Zealand (a division of Pearson New Zealand Ltd.) •
Penguin Books (South Africa) (Pty.) Ltd., 24 Sturdee Avenue, Rosebank, Johannesburg 2196,
South Africa

Penguin Books Ltd., Registered Offices: 80 Strand, London WC2R 0RL, England

While the author has made every effort to provide accurate telephone numbers, Internet addresses,
and other contact information at the time of publication, neither the publisher nor the author
assumes any responsibility for errors, or for changes that occur after publication. Further, the
publisher does not have any control over and does not assume any responsibility for author or third-
party websites or their content.

HANDWRITTEN RECIPES

First edition: October 2012

ISBN: 978-0-399-16014-1

An application to catalog this book has been submitted to the Library of Congress.

PRINTED IN THE UNITED STATES OF AMERICA

10 9 8 7 6 5 4 3 2 1

The recipes contained in this book are to be followed exactly as written. The publisher is not
responsible for your specific health or allergy needs that may require medical supervision. The
publisher is not responsible for any adverse reactions to the recipes contained in this book.

Most Perigee books are available at special quantity discounts for bulk purchases for sales
promotions, premiums, fund-raising, or educational use. Special books, or book excerpts, can also
be created to fit specific needs. For details, write: Special Markets, Penguin Group (USA) Inc.,
375 Hudson Street, New York, New York 10014.

ALWAYS LEARNING   PEARSON

For Ramona

Contents

Main Dishes
73

Barbecued Beef ✷ Chef Meat Sauce ✷ Ham 'n' Lamb
Kabobs ✷ Stuffed Peppers ✷ Italian Pie ✷ Meat and
Cheese Loaf ✷ Lamb Loaf ✷ Meat Ball Mexicana ✷ Sweet
and Sour Pork ✷ Chicken Legs ✷ Scalloped Salmon with
Noodles and Almonds ✷ Tuna Croquettes ✷ Chicken and
Spaghetti Casserole ✷ Spaghetti Sauce ✷ Red Pepper
Quiche ✷ Pasta with Artichokes, Capers, and Tomatoes

Desserts
109

Blonde Brownies ✷ Paul's Pumpkin Bars ✷ Almond
Christmas Balls ✷ Cherry Walnut Bars ✷ Cloud Nine
Butterscotch Bars ✷ Maple Sugar ✷ Kolocki ✷ Italian
Cookies ✷ Mince Meat Cookies ✷ Molasses
Popcorn Balls ✷ Date Torte Cookies ✷ Praline
Wafers ✷ Springerle ✷ Dutch Apple Cake ✷ Jewish
Apple Cake ✷ Applesauce Cake ✷ Praline Applesauce
Cake ✷ Fruit Cake ✷ Boston Prune Cake ✷ Butterscotch
Yule Log ✷ Chocolate Porcupine ✷ English
Plum Pudding ✷ Orange Kiss-Me Cake ✷ Fudge
Cake ✷ Pineapple Chiffon Cake ✷ Simple Pound
Cake ✷ Butter Scotch Pie ✷ Green Tomato Pie ✷ Caramel
Custard Pie ✷ Fresh Fruit Ice Cream Pie ✷ Prune
Meringue Pie ✷ Apricot Bavarian Cream ✷ Rice Dainty
Peach Smoothee ✷ Coconut Dreams

Thanks
193

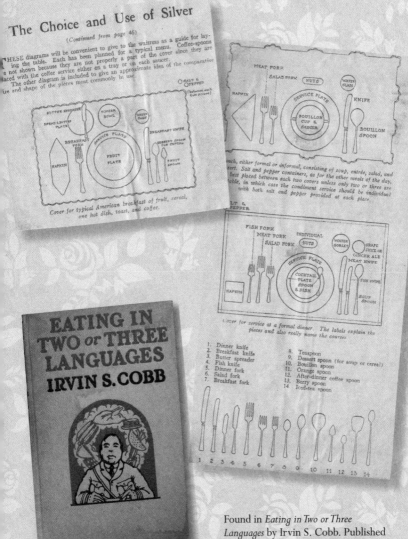

Found in *Eating in Two or Three Languages* by Irvin S. Cobb. Published by George H. Doran, 1919.

Introduction

First, let's get things straight. I'm a bookseller, not a cook. Sure, there are a few dishes I enjoy making, but I'm not one of those people who goes crazy without something in the oven. What makes me qualified to put together a collection of recipes? Leaf through your cookbooks, and you're likely to find a bit of paper with a recipe written in a familiar (or not-so-familiar) hand. It could be a family secret finally divulged, a scribbled interpretation of something seen on TV, even a culinary experiment long since forgotten. What happens to these recipes when the books are passed on? That's where I come in.

With 70,000 books and 3,000 cookbooks in stock in my bookshop and thousands more that have passed through my hands, I've come across many of these artifacts. Over the years, I've recovered nearly 500 recipes, many of which I've posted to my blogs, *Forgotten Bookmarks* and *Handwritten Recipes*. When selecting the ones for this book, I chose recipes that represent the variety of what I've found.

I make no claims about the taste, ease of preparation, or completeness of these recipes. They were chosen because they looked interesting. Sometimes that interest came from thinking a recipe sounded delicious, sometimes it came from morbid curiosity (people really ate this stuff?), and a few were chosen simply because the handwriting was clear. Some are not handwritten, but they appeared to be typed up or photocopied, and that seemed okay to me. When a recipe seemed a little too vague or poorly written, I tried to fill in any essential or obvious information. Many of these recipes are incomplete or written in an unknown shorthand, and I tried to leave the originals intact as much as possible. You're on your own to unlock the secrets, which, in my opinion, is as much fun as eating the results.

After spending time with these books and recipes, I was surprised by both the variety and creativity. Most of these came from the 1930s through 1950s, and I imagined I would find a lot of gelatin molds and casseroles. I certainly found both, but I also found some classic ethnic dishes like kolocki, Italian-style cookies, springerle, and "Granapfla"—which I discovered is actually the classic German dumpling dish knepfla. There are muffins with bacon, scalloped tomatoes, salmon with almonds, kabobs, red pepper quiche, and, yes, a few casserole dishes. The collection is heavy on desserts; for every main dish I'd find between the pages, there seemed to be ten recipes for peanut butter cookies.

Due to my lack of culinary skills, I have asked a few fellow bloggers to try out some of the recipes and provide some photographic context for these often mysterious concoctions. Other than that, I have let the recipes stand alone. It's up to you to decide if you are brave enough to try them. I hope you find the collection to be a different look at food at the very least, and that you perhaps find a new go-to recipe in the bunch.

An Advertisement for Knapp's Good Food of Garberville, California

Found in *Old English Ballads*
by Francis Gummere.
Published by Ginn and Co.,
1899.

Breads and Baked Goods

Graham Bread
½ cup sugar   dash salt
½ cup molasses   1 teas.
2 tbl. shortening
2 cups sour milk } dissolve
1 heaping teas. soda
1 cup sweet milk
1 teas baking powder.
2 cups graham flour
1 cup wheat flour

Makes two loaves.
Mix flour, + powder, sugar,
salt, lard, molasses, sour
milk + soda, sweet milk.

COOK BOOK

Sponsored by
ST. PAUL'S SUNDAY EVENING GROUP

ST. PAUL'S CHURCH
CONCORD, N.H.

Found in *St. Paul's Sunday Evening Group Cook Book*. Published by St. Paul's Church, Concord, NH, 1935.

GRAHAM BREAD

⮫

½ cup sugar

dash of salt (1 teaspoon)

½ cup molasses

2 tablespoons shortening

2 cups sour milk

1 heaping teaspoon baking soda

1 cup sweet milk

1 teaspoon baking powder

2 cups graham flour

1 cup wheat flour

Dissolve baking soda in sour milk. Mix flour, baking powder, sugar, salt, shortening, molasses, sour milk plus baking soda, and sweet milk.

Makes two loaves.

SOUTHERN BELL BREAD

½ tablespoon dry yeast
1 cup lukewarm water (pot water)
⅛ cup honey
1 cup mashed potato (?)
½ cup rice flour
¼ cup sesame seeds
¼ cup soy flour
1 tablespoon grits
½ teaspoon salt
½ cup rice flour
⅛ cup oil

Combine yeast, water, and honey. Add potato, rice flour, and sesame seeds to yeast mixture; let stand 1½ hours.

When risen, stir in soy flour, grits, salt, rice flour, and oil. Knead until dough is elastic. Rise again, covered, for 1 hour or until doubled.

Stir dough down. Knead to shape loaf. Place in oiled pan. Rise again until nearly doubled. Bake at 350 degrees for 30 minutes.

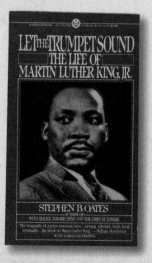

Found in *Let the Trumpet Sound: The Life of Martin Luther King Jr.* by Stephen B. Oates. Published by Mentor, 1985.

½ TBS. DRY YEAST
(POT WATER)
1 C LUKE WARM WATER
⅛ c HONEY

1 c M'D. POT.
½ c RICE FLOUR   ⎫   ADD TO YST
¼ c SESAME SEEDS   ⎬   MIXT. —
                            3 ½ hr.

¼ c SOY FLOUR
1½ TBS. GRITS
2 TSP. SALT   WHEN RISEN
½ c. RICE FLOUR   STIR IN THESE.
                          KNEAD TIL
⅛ c. OIL   DOUGH IS ELASTIC.
                       RISE AGAIN COV'D 1 HR
                          OR TIL DBLD.

STIR DOUGH DOWN. KNEAD TO SHAPE
LOAF. OIL'D PAN. RISE AGAIN
TIL NEARLY DBL'D.

350° 30 MIN.

Brown Bread.

2/3 cup Molasses
1 cup sugar } beat together

2 eggs

1 teasp salt
  cup flour (White) } stir in flour
3 cups graham flour   salt
  tsp baking soda } put 1 tsp soda
2 cups Buttermilk   in 1 cup milk

Bake about 45 minutes at 356°

Found in *Good Night, Sweet Prince* by Gene Fowler.
Published by the Viking Press, 1944.

BROWN BREAD

⚬⚬⚬

⅔ cup molasses
1 cup sugar
2 eggs
1 teaspoon salt
1 cup flour (white)
3 cups graham flour
2 teaspoons baking soda
2 cups buttermilk

Beat together molasses, sugar, and eggs. Stir in flour and salt.

Put 1 teaspoon soda in 1 cup buttermilk, each.

Combine and bake about 45 minutes at 350.

Light Bread

⤠

3 cups milk

¾ cup sugar

2 teaspoons salt

1 tablespoon butter

1 yeast cake, dissolved in ½ cup lukewarm water

3 quarts flour, or enough to make stiff dough

Scald milk. In a large bowl, combine milk, sugar, salt, and butter.

Cool and add yeast-water mixture. Sift in flour.

Knead dough smooth and set to rise in a warm place, about 84 degrees.

When it has doubled in bulk, turn onto a floured board and knead lightly. Shape into loaves; place in pans and rise again.

Bake in moderate oven, 325 or 350 degrees, for about an hour.

Now, Berniece, be sure your loaf pans are well buttered so that the minute the bread is done you can turn the loaves out to cool on a rack. You can halve this recipe, or do like I do, make it all and either freeze some of the loaves, or go ahead and cook them and freeze the extra baked bread.

"Receipt" for "Light Bread"...

...ald 3 cups of milk; add (in a large bowl) to 3/4ths
...up sugar, 2 teaspoons of salt and 1 tablespoon of butter.
...ool and add a yeast cake, dissolved in 1/2 cup lukewarm
...ater. Sift in 3 quarts of flour (enough to make dough
...tiff). Knead smooth, set to rise in a warm place (about
...4° will do it); when it has doubled in bulk turn onto a
...lour board and knead lightly. Shape into loaves; place
...n pans and set to rise again. Bake in moderate oven
...350° or 325°) about an hour.

Now, Berniece, be sure your loaf pans are well buttered so
that the minute the bread is done you can turn the loaves
...ut to cool on a rack. You can halve this recipe, or do
like I do, make it all and either freeze some of the loaves,
or go ahead and cook them and freeze the extra baked bread.

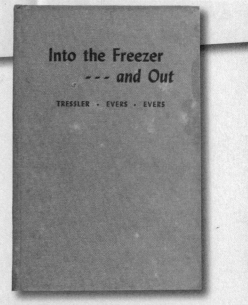

Into the Freezer
--- and Out

TRESSLER · EVERS · EVERS

Found in *Into the Freezer—and Out*
by Donald K. Tressler, Clifford F.
Evers, and Barbara Hutchings
Evers. Published by the Avi
Publishing Co., 1953.

Corn Muffins or
Corn Bread

1½ C corn Meal
½ C Flour
2   4 tsp Baking Pwd
⅓ tsp salt
1 egg beaten
1 bsp sugar
¼ C oil or fat
¼ 1 C milk

Beat egg
add milk &
oil beat. Add
flour cornmeal
salt B Powder
sugar

Bake
at 425°
20 min.
greased
pans -

Corn Muffins or Corn Bread

❧

1 ½ cups cornmeal
½ cup flour
4 teaspoons baking powder
½ teaspoon salt
1 egg, beaten
1 tablespoon sugar
¼ cup oil or fat
1 cup milk

Beat egg. Add milk and oil; beat. Add flour, cornmeal, salt, baking powder, and sugar.

Bake at 425 degrees, 20 minutes, greased pans.

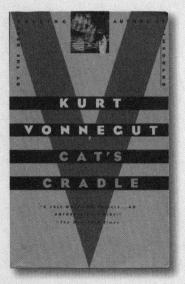

Found in *Cat's Cradle* by Kurt Vonnegut.
Published by Dell, 1998.

CRANBERRY NUT BREAD RING

3 *cups flour*

3½ *teaspoons baking powder*

½ *teaspoon baking soda*

1 *teaspoon salt*

⅔ *cup sugar*

⅓ *cup shortening*

1 *egg, beaten*

¾ *cup milk*

1 *cup cranberry-orange relish*

1 *cup chopped pecans*

Heat oven to 350.

Sift first five ingredients together. Cut in shortening. Add egg and milk. Stir in relish and pecans. Put in tube pan and bake for 55 to 60 minutes. Cool for 10 minutes in pan.

Found in *Physical Culture Cook Book* by Bernarr MacFadden. Published by MacFadden Publications, 1924.

Cranberry Nut Bread Ring

3 cups flour
3½ tsp Baking powder
½ tsp Soda
1 tsp Salt
⅔ cup Sugar
⅓ cup Shortening
1 Egg, beaten
¾ cup milk
1 cup Cranberry-Orange Relish
1 cup chopped pecans.
Oven 350° - 55-60 min.

Sift 1-5   Stir in 9 & 10
Cut in 6   Put in tube pan
Add 7 & 8   & bake 55-60
                     Cool 10 min in Pan

Pineapple Date Bread

1 beaten egg
½ cup milk
⅓ cup melted shortening or salad oil.
1. 9 oz can or 1 cup crushed pineapple
1 cup chopped walnuts
1 cup " dates
3 cups flour
3/4 cup sugar
3 teas. baking powder
3/4 " salt
1/4 " soda

Combine egg, milk, shortening, pineapple, nuts and dates
Sift dry ingredients and add to first mixture and
stir just to moisten. Bake in greased 9½ x 5 x 3" loaf
pan in 350° for 55 min.

PINEAPPLE DATE BREAD

1 beaten egg
⅓ cup milk
⅓ cup melted shortening or salad oil
1 (9-ounce) can or 1 cup crushed pineapple
1 cup chopped walnuts
1 cup chopped dates
3 cups flour
¾ cup sugar
3 teaspoons baking powder
¾ teaspoon salt
¼ teaspoon baking soda

Combine egg, milk, shortening, pineapple, nuts, and dates.

Sift dry ingredients together separately and add to first mixture. Stir fruit to moisten.

Bake in greased 9½-by-5-by-3-inch loaf pan in 350-degree oven for 55 minutes.

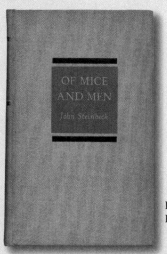

Found in *Of Mice and Men* by John Steinbeck.
Published by Covici Friede, 1937.

HARVEST LOAF

❧

1 ¾ cups flour
1 teaspoon baking soda
1 teaspoon cinnamon
salt
½ teaspoon nutmeg
¼ teaspoon ginger
¼ teaspoon cloves
½ cup oleo
1 cup sugar
2 eggs
¾ cup pumpkin
¾ cup chocolate chips
¾ cup nuts

Grease pan. Combine all ingredients. Bake for approximately 30 minutes at 350 degrees.

Harvest Loaf.
1 ¾ c flour
1 t. soda
1 t. cinn.
salt
½ t nutmeg
¼ t. ginger
¼ t. cloves
½ c oleo
1 c sugar
2 eggs
¾ c pumpkin
¾ c choc chips
¾ c nuts
Grease pan - bake
approx 30 min @ 350°

Found in *Guilty as Sin* by Tami Hoag.
Published by Bantam Books, 2004.

Zucchini Bread

2 cups grated zucchini w/
the juice

2 cups Sugar
1 cup oil
3 eggs
1 tsp Vanilla

mix:

Then add: 3 cups flour
   1/4 tsp power
   1 tsp soda
   1/2 tsp salt
   1 tsp cinammon
   1 Tsp ginger
   1 tsp ground cloves

mix well: grease & flour
2 loaf pans   Bake 350° - 1 hour

Zucchini Bread

2 cups grated zucchini with the juice
2 cups sugar
1 cup oil
3 eggs
1 teaspoon vanilla
3 cups flour
¼ teaspoon (baking) powder
1 teaspoon (baking) soda
½ teaspoon salt
1 teaspoon cinnamon
1 teaspoon ginger
1 teaspoon ground cloves

Mix together zucchini, sugar, oil, eggs, and vanilla.

Add flour, baking powder, baking soda, salt, and spices. Mix well.

Grease and flour 2 loaf pans. Bake at 350F for 1 hour.

Found in *365 Ways to Cook Hamburger* by
Doyne Nickerson. Published by
Doubleday & Co., 1960.

Maple Syrup Doughnuts
1 cup maple syrup
2 Eggs
3 tbl shortening
½ tsp salt
1 tsp soda
1 tsp Baking Powder
½ tsp nutmeg
2 tsp Vanilla
⅔ cup sour milk
Flour to make ~~workable~~
dough. Mix ingredients as
stated adding enough
to make dough workable
Pat out on floured
½ inch thickness +
doughnut cutter
hot fat +

Polish Doughnuts
dissolve 1 yeast cake
1 pint of milk which
has been scalded + coole
Add 2 cups flour. Let
stand in warm place ½ h
Beat 4 egg yolks + 1 egg wl
½ cup sugar, tsp salt,
½ tsp Vanilla + grated rind
of lemon or orange. Add to
yeast with ½ cup melted butter
Add 5 cups flour cover + let
rise until double in bulk.
Turn on floured board + pat
till ½ inch thickness. Cut
with doughnut cutter, Cover
+ let rise until light + fry
in deep, hot fat.

MAPLE SYRUP DOUGHNUTS

1 cup maple syrup

2 eggs

3 tablespoons shortening

½ teaspoon salt

1 teaspoon soda

1 teaspoon baking powder

½ teaspoon nutmeg

1 teaspoon vanilla

⅔ cup sour milk

flour to make workable dough

Mix ingredients as stated, adding enough flour to make dough workable.

Pat out on floured board to ½ inch thickness and cut with doughnut cutter. Fry in hot fat, heated to 370 degrees.

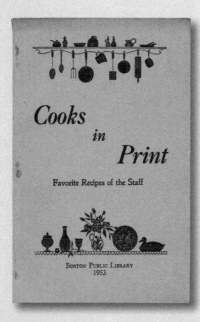

Found in *Cooks in Print* by the staff of the Boston Public Library. Published by the Boston Public Library, 1953.

POLISH DOUGHNUTS

1 yeast cake
1 pint milk, scalded and cooled
7 cups flour, divided
4 egg yolks
1 egg
½ cup sugar
1 teaspoon salt
½ teaspoon vanilla
grated rind of 1 lemon or orange
½ cup melted butter

Dissolve yeast cake in scalded milk. Add 2 cups flour. Let stand in warm place for ½ hour.

Beat egg yolks and egg with sugar, salt, vanilla, and lemon or orange rind. Add to yeast with melted butter. Add remaining flour. Cover and let rise until doubled in bulk.

Turn on floured board and pat until ½ inch thickness. Cut with doughnut cutter. Cover and let rise until light. Fry in deep, hot fat.

Peanut-Butter Cereal Muffins

❧

1½ cups flour
3 teaspoons baking powder
½ teaspoon salt
½ cup creamy or chunk-style peanut butter
¼ cup margarine
⅓ cup brown sugar
1 egg
1 cup milk
1½ cups whole wheat flakes, crushed, to make 1 cup crumbled
4 slices crisp bacon, crumbled (optional)
½ teaspoon cinnamon

Sift flour, baking powder, salt.

Beat peanut butter, margarine, ¼ cup brown sugar, and egg. Add flour with milk. Add crumbs and bacon; mix until moistened. Spoon in greased muffin pans. Add brown sugar and cinnamon and milk. Sprinkle over muffin batter.

400-degree oven, 18–20 min.

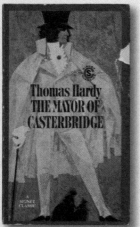

Found in *The Mayor of Casterbridge* by Thomas Hardy. Published by Signet Classics, 1962.

Peanut-Butter Cereal Muffins

1½ cups flour
3 tsp. Baking powder
½ tsp salt
⅔ cup creamy or chunk-style peanut Butter
¼ cup margarine
½ cup Brown sugar
3 egg   1 cup milk
1½ cup whole wheat flakes crushed to make 1 cup crumbs.
4 slices crisp bacon crumbled
½ tsp cinnamon (optional)

Sift flour, baking powder, salt
Beat peanut butter, margarine
1 cup Brown sugar & egg. Add flour
with milk. add crumbs & bacon, mix
until moistened. Spoon in greased muffin
pans. Add brown sugar & cinnamon + mix
Sprinkle over muffin batter.
400° oven 18-50 m

Lindsey Meys blogs about cupcakes and other sweet treats at *Sugar Heaven* (http://lickthespoonbaking.blogspot.com). She's also my sister. I didn't have any cupcake recipes for her to try out, but this seemed like the next best thing. Here's her take on them:

Peanut butter and breakfast. My two favorite things—combined into one delicious confection? I had to try this recipe. Everything about these muffins seemed straightforward, but whoever wrote this recipe must have been joking about bacon being "optional." If bacon is an option to be used in a recipe, it's not optional—it's essential.

The batter looked delicious after adding the bacon, but I got caught off guard by the streusel topping. I had already used the brown sugar and milk—uh-oh! So I threw together about ⅓ cup of brown sugar, 1 tablespoon of milk, and the ½ teaspoon cinnamon to make a streusel-like topping for the muffins and spooned it over the top of each.

After 5 minutes of cooling time, I unwrapped these bacon- and peanut butter–filled delicacies and the verdict is . . . delicious! I can taste the wheat cereal, I can taste the bacon, I can taste the streusel topping—I can taste everything that went into this little muffin. It is delicious, moist, and filling! You could definitely add nuts or even chocolate chips to it, and it would add a whole new dimension. Great recipe—I am definitely adding it to my recipe book.

LINDSEY MEYS

Sour Cream Coffee Cake

1 cup sugar
½ cup butter or shortening
2 eggs
1 cup sour cream
1 teaspoon vanilla
2 cups flour
1 teaspoon baking powder
1 teaspoon baking soda

Cream butter. Add sugar and eggs. Then add dry ingredients. Add sour cream.

Pour half of batter in a greased pan and sprinkle with half of filling (recipe follows). Pour in remaining batter; top with remaining filling.

Bake at 350 degrees for 25 to 30 minutes.

FILLING

1 cup brown sugar
3 tablespoons sifted flour
1 teaspoon cinnamon
3 tablespoons butter
1 cup chopped nuts
raisins (optional)

Combine all ingredients.

Found in *Less Than Zero* by Bret Easton Ellis. Published by Simon & Schuster, 1985.

Sour Cream Coffee Cake

1 cup sugar
1/2 cup butter or shorting
2 eggs
1 cup sour cream
1 tsp Vanilla
2 cups flour
1 tsp B. Powder
1 tsp B. soda

Bake 350
for 25 or 30
mins

Cream butter Add sugar
And eggs then Add dry
Ings add sour cream
Pour half batter in greased
pan + sprinkle with ½ feeling
Pour in remaining batter
with remaing feeling
feeling

1 cup brown sugar
3 tbs sifted flour
1 tsp ~~vanilla~~ Cinnamon
3 tbs butter
cup chopped nuts

raisins
maybe
Added

Nai to' yuons 45 jectei

Baking Powder Biscuits —
2 Cups Flour — 4 Tsp. Baking Powder — 1/2 Tsp Salt — 3/4 Cup Milk
4 Tbsp. shortening — —Method — Sift Flour, Baking —
Powder and Salt Together Rub shortening in with
Fingertips, Add Milk slowly and Mix to a Soft
dough, Roll out on a slightly Floured board
to a half inch thickness — cut with a biscuit
cutter, Bake in Quick oven (450°F.) 10—15
Minutes, Yield, 12 Biscuits

This Season's
COOK BOOK
10¢ No. 1

HUNDREDS of RECIPES
for
UNUSUAL DISHES
•
SEASONABLE MENUS
USEFUL CHARTS

BAKING POWDER BISCUITS

2 cups flour
4 teaspoons baking powder
½ teaspoon salt
¾ cup milk
4 tablespoons shortening

Sift flour, baking powder, and salt together. Rub shortening in with fingertips. Add milk slowly and mix to a soft dough. Roll out on a slightly floured board. Cut with a biscuit cutter. Bake in quick oven (450 degrees), 10 to 15 minutes. Yield: 12 biscuits.

Found in *This Season's Cook Book, vol. 1, no. 1* (no author).
Published by the Dell Publishing Co., 1938.

Sour Milk Biscuit

∽

2 cups (graham?) flour

1 teaspoon baking powder

½ teaspoon soda

1 teaspoon salt

¼ cup shortening

⅔ cup sour milk

Combine dry ingredients. Stir in milk. Knead lightly. Bake at 450 degrees, 10 to 12 minutes.

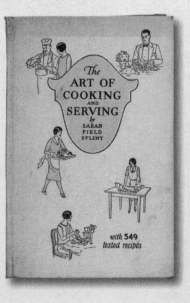

Found in *The Art of Cooking and Serving* by Sarah Field Splint. Published by Procter & Gamble, 1930.

Sour Milk Biscuit

2 C. g. m flour   1 tsp salt

1 tsp. B.P.   ¼ C shortening

½ tsp soda

Stir in ⅔ C sour milk

knead lightly

Bake 450°   10 to 12 min,

UNIVERSAL WAFFLES

~

2 cups flour
2 cups milk
1 teaspoon salt
2 eggs
3 teaspoons baking powder
4 tablespoons butter

Sift flour, salt, and baking powder into mixing bowl.

Beat yolks of eggs well into milk. Add a little at a time, beating all until perfectly smooth. Then add butter. Have egg whites beaten stiff and fold into mixture.

Have waffle iron hot before you start using it.

This is a large rule. Half makes enough for a company of four.

PASTE FOR CLEANING IRON

2 tablespoons baking soda
1 teaspoon water

Brush iron grids. Do not do this often. Never wash grids after using, as it sticks.

Universal Waffles –

2 cups flour.
2 " milk.   1 tsp salt.
3 eggs.   3 " B. Powd.
4 tbs butter.

Sift flour, salt, B. Powd, into
mixing bowl. Beat yolks of eggs
well into milk add little at a
time beating all till perfectly
smooth. Then add butter, have
egg whites beaten stiff and fold
into mixture,

Have waffle iron hot before you
start using it,

This is a large rule & makes
enough for a company of four.
paste for cleaning iron.
tbs soda, 1 tsp water, Brush iron grids so
it sticks
not do this after, never wash grids after
using

In my house, waffles are a Sunday tradition. The recipe started out as a simple one from *The Tassajara Bread Book*, but has been heavily adapted over the years. New ingredients have been added, quantities changed, and the balance of dry and wet, sweet and savory, has been tweaked to achieve the perfect waffle. So we decided to try this recipe out ourselves.

This "large rule" makes a nice loose batter, stiffened by the inclusion of beaten egg whites. Since the recipe doesn't specify when to combine the dry and wet ingredients, we did it after beating in the whites. We also added the melted butter directly to the eggs, then added the milk, knowing that it's easier to get fats to combine when there's no other liquid in the mix.

The resulting waffle was consummately crisp and dry, very light and not too "eggy." The large dose of butter makes for a rich, toothsome outer crust. But the author is a little off base about the serving size, at least by our modern standards. You could serve four with the full recipe, but not with half, unless you want to send people away hungry.

Michael Popek

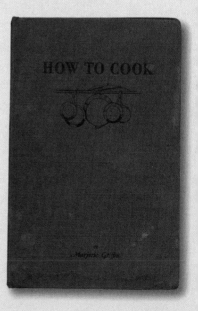

Found in *How to Cook* by Marjorie Griffin.
Published by Hall Publishing Co., 1944.

Found in *Kill As
Directed* by Ellery
Queen. Published by
Pocket Books, 1963.

Side
Dishes

Spring Salad

~

1 hard-boiled egg, sliced
16 spears cooked asparagus
1 tomato, sliced
⅓ cup diced celery
¼ cup chopped green pepper
1 tablespoon finely chopped onion
½ teaspoon salt
¼ teaspoon paprika
4 pieces lettuce

Chill all ingredients and combine. Place on lettuce leaves. Serve with Roquefort dressing (recipe follows).

Roquefort Dressing

¼ cup Roquefort cheese
1 teaspoon sugar
½ teaspoon salt
¼ teaspoon celery seed
¼ teaspoon paprika
2 tablespoons lemon juice
4 tablespoons salad oil

Cream cheese with fork. Add remaining ingredients and chill. Serve on chilled salad.

Serves four.

Spring Salad Serving four
1 hard cooked egg sliced.
16 spears cooked aspargus
1 tomato sliced
⅓ cup diced celery
¼ " chopped green pepper
1 tbs finely chopped onion
½ tsp Salt ¼ tsp paprika
4 pieces lettuce.
Chill all ingredience and combine
place on lettuce leaves Serve with
    Roquefort dressing.
¼ cup roquefort cheese 1 tsp Sugar
½ tsp salt ¼ tsp celery seed ¼ tsp paprika
2 tbs lemon juice 4 tbs salad oil
cream cheese with fork add rest of
ingredients and chill, serve on chilled
Salad.

Found in *Cap'n Dan's Daughter* by
Joseph C. Lincoln. Published by
A. L. Burt, 1914.

Cranberry Salad

1 c Cranberries (cut or ground)
1 c sugar   1 sm pkg Lemon Jello
1 c Hot Water   1 c Pineapple Juice
Combine & chill in Bowl until syrupy
Add 1 c chopped Celery
1 c pineapple drained   ½ c chopped Nuts
Pour into mold & serve

CRANBERRY SALAD

❧

1 cup cranberries (cut or ground)
1 cup sugar
1 small package of lemon Jell-O
1 cup hot water
1 cup pineapple juice

Combine and chill in bowl until syrupy.

Add:

1 cup chopped celery
1 cup pineapple, drained
½ cup chopped nuts

Pour into mold and serve.

Found in *How I Cook It* by
Virginia McDonald. Published
by Frank Glenn Publishing, 1949.

Zuchini Salad

$\frac{1}{4}$ c. onion flakes + 3 tbl water (let stand 10 min)
2 medium zuchini unpeeled
2 cukes   peeled
$\frac{1}{4}$ c. sugar
1 tbl tsp. salt
1 c. white vinegar
$\frac{3}{4}$ $\frac{1}{2}$ tsp. pepper
$\frac{1}{2}$ tsp. red pepper (crushed)
$\frac{1}{4}$ tsp. garlic powder

Alternate veg. in bowl. Slice thin. dissolve sugar
+ salt - 1 c. hot water + add rest of ingredients
Mix well + pour over veg. Cover + refrigrat
at least 1 hr before serving.

Zucchini Salad

¼ cup onion flakes

3 tablespoons water

2 medium zucchini, unpeeled

2 cucumbers, peeled

¼ cup sugar

1 teaspoon salt

1 cup hot water

1 cup white vinegar

½ teaspoon pepper

½ teaspoon red pepper, crushed

¼ teaspoon garlic powder

Combine onion flakes and water. Let stand 10 minutes.

Alternate vegetables in a bowl, sliced thin. Dissolve sugar and salt in hot water. Add rest of ingredients to water. Mix well and pour over vegetables. Cover and refrigerate for at least 1 hour before serving.

Found in *Fun to Cook Book* by Margie Blake.
Published by Carnation Co., 1955.

FRENCH KRAUT

❧

1 pound onions (4)

2 quarts cabbage

4 peppers, red and green

1 small can pimientos

⅔ cup vinegar

1 cup sugar

1 tablespoon celery seed

⅔ tablespoons allspice

Heat and let cool. Mix and let set overnight.

Found in *La France Nouvelle* by
L. Raymond Talbot. Published
by Benjamin H. Sanborn and
Co., 1921.

French Kraut.

1 # onions (4)
2 pts. cabbage
4 peppers 2 red
3 green
small can pimentos.

2/3 cup vinegar
1 cup sugar
1 tbsp. celery seed
2/3 tbsp. allspice—

heat & let cool
mix & let set over
night.

FRIED SPINACH

~

After you have fried meat such as veal steak, pork chops, or round steak, cut up one clove of garlic in same frying pan and brown. Then add one can of spinach and let simmer for a few minutes.

Found in *A Moveable Feast* by Ernest
Hemingway. Published by Bantam, 1965.

Fried Spinach.

After you have fried meat such as veal steak, pork chops or round steak, cut up 1 clove of garlic in same frying pan & brown. Then add 1 can of spinach & let simmer for a few minutes.

The sensational #1 bestseller
By the author of *A FAREWELL TO ARMS* and
THE OLD MAN AND THE SEA

A BANTAM NINETY-FIVE ★ 95¢ ★ N3048

ERNEST HEMINGWAY'S
A MOVEABLE FEAST

The wild young years of the Lost Generation in Paris

"Hemingway at his best...savagely written, full of love and bitterness."
The New York Times

SCALLOPED TOMATOES

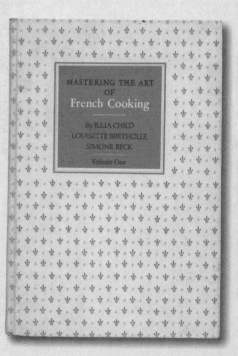

1 pint tomatoes
1 pint bread crumbs
2 tablespoons butter
1 tablespoon sugar
2 teaspoons salt
1 teaspoon pepper

Alternate layers of tomatoes and bread crumbs. Season each layer and cover with small pieces of butter. Finish with crumbs on top. Bake for a half hour.

Found in *Mastering the Art of French Cooking, vol. 1* by Julia Child, Louisette Bertholle, and Simone Beck. Published by Alfred A. Knopf, 1971.

Scalloped Tomatoes

1 pint tomatoes
1 pint Bread crumbs
2 tablespoons Butter
2 "   "   sugar
2 teaspoons salt
1 saltspoon pepper

Alternate layers of tomatoes +
bread crumbs, season each
layer + cover with small pieces
of butter. Crumbs on top. Bake
half hour.

Eggs in a Basket

6 hard-cooked eggs
1 can deviled ham
1 tablespoon mayonnaise
1 tablespoon sweet pickle relish.
Green pepper, pimiento, stuffed olives.
Cut eggs in half & remove yolks.
Blend ham, mayonnaise & relish
Fill hollows with mixture & garnish
with strips of pepper, pimientos &
stuffed olives.

Found in *Good Egg Dishes* by
Ambrose Heath. Published by
Faber and Faber Ltd., 1952.

Eggs in a Basket

6 hard-cooked eggs
1 can deviled ham
1 tablespoon mayonnaise
1 tablespoon sweet pickle relish
green pepper, pimiento, stuffed olives (chopped into strips)

Cut eggs in half and remove yolks.

Blend ham, mayonnaise and relish.

Fill hollows with mixture and garnish with strips of pepper, pimiento, and stuffed olives.

Granappfla—

Take as much flour as You
think You will want for the
amt— add 1 egg— little salt—
stir with milk till rather soft
dough is formed. then have
some boiling water, into this
from end of spoon scrape very
little pieces in the water keep
—/- boiling all the time, cook
well for a few min, skim ou
cover with bread crumbs
when cool fry till a nice br
[fried onions can be put on top
this is a matter of choice]

Louise Damm——
Sennee Falls.

GRANAPFLA
(KNEPFLA, GERMAN DUMPLINGS)

flour
1 egg
salt
milk
bread crumbs

Take as much flour as you think you will want for the amount. Add egg and a little salt. Stir with milk until a rather soft dough is formed.

There have some boiling water. Into this, from the end of a spoon, scrape very little pieces of dough in the water. Keep it boiling all the time.

Cook well for a few minutes, then skim out and cover with bread crumbs.

When cool, fry until a nice brown. Fried onions can be put on top—this is a matter of choice.

Louise Hammer, Seneca Falls

Found in *Women's Institute of Cookery* (no author). Published by the Women's Institute of Domestic Arts and Sciences, 1927.

I sent this recipe to Nick Livermore, who runs the blog *Frugal Feeding* (http://frugalfeeding.com). I love his no-nonsense approach to cooking and baking, and I thought this recipe for simple dumplings was right up his alley. I'll let him explain the philosophy behind *Frugal Feeding* and what he thought about this recipe:

> *It is a well-documented fact that the vast proportion of those enrolled at university tends toward financial strife. The nefarious lures and vices of higher education, which seem only too inevitable, wreak indiscriminate havoc among wallets and purses alike. As such, I found myself lost in the sea of a sizable overdraft. This situation, though a little exaggerated and certainly not irretrievable, combined with a love of both food and writing, eventually prompted the foundation of my blog,* Frugal Feeding. *One is always loathed, when short of the necessary currency, to part with more money that any given situation requires, and it soon became apparent that eating "on the cheap" was tremendously easy. The problem with this is that doing so tends to be incredibly dull, not to mention the fact that it tends to avoid compromise with the same vim used to evade the plague. If I may be so bold as to make use of an American colloquialism, the basic premise of* Frugal Feeding, *to help people achieve gastronomic greatness without compromise, was a complete "no-brainer."*
>
> *Knepfla, a rather basic version of the humble dumpling, are an indigene of Germany. Indeed, they appear to be reminiscent of the particularly frugal living central Europe was once known for. Unlike the style of dumpling commonly found on the British Isles, these contain no fat—that is, no butter, lard, or suet. Such an omission benefits the knepfla in a number of ways, making them at once simple, quick, and cheap to produce.*
>
> *As you can see, the recipe I was provided with was a little bare-bones. Thankfully, however, it was also fairly self-explanatory. In the end, the quantities used were 200 grams plain flour, 1 egg, roughly 100 milliliters of milk, and a generous pinch of salt. This mixture produced enough dough for between 10 and 15 dumplings. The quantity of milk is stated as being rough simply because no two batches of flour behave in exactly the same manner; it would be best*

to add it little by little. On the subject of milk, it seems that many recipes for knepfla substitute milk for water. However, in terms of flavor and texture, this is probably inadvisable, in the same way as making porridge in a similar fashion is. You see, the use of milk goes some way toward mitigating the lack of butter.

Despite the use of milk, the taste of these dumplings is rather different than those found elsewhere. As has been mentioned above, such an omission has what can only be described as a negative on this aspect of their character; they are rather stolid, dense, and heavy. However, they fulfill rather well the purpose for which they were originally devised: to fill the stomach of some poor, old Germanic sod. Unfortunately, the lack of fat also means that they taste of very little. Yet this is only true of the dumplings in their traditional form. The additional process of frying lifts their flavor profile a little, particularly if it is performed using olive oil. They appear to be best served as a snack or aperitif with a dip or sauce such as mayonnaise. If serving without the bread crumbs, then a soup or bisque may be seen to benefit from their presence, depending on one's taste in dumpling.

NICK LIVERMORE

LEMON RICE

⌘

½ cup rice
2 eggs, separated
juice and rind of 1 lemon
2 cups milk
¾ cup sugar

Cook rice in salt water until tender. Drain and pour cold water over. Do not stir, just drain.

Add egg yolks, grated lemon rind and milk. Put into dish and bake in a moderate oven until done. Remove from oven and let cool.

Beat egg whites until stiff. Add lemon juice and sugar. Spread on top and bake this for about ¾ hour. Try with a silver knife—if clean, it is done. Bake as a custard. This forms sort of a jelly with the rice.

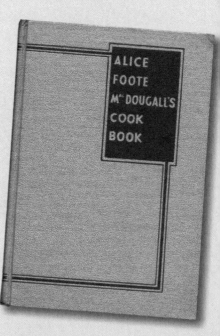

Found in *Alice Foote MacDougall's Cook Book* by Alice Foote MacDougall. Published by Lothrop, Lee, and Shepard, 1935.

This serves about 6 people

Lemon Rice

¾ cup rice cooked in salt
water till tender drain and
pour cold water over do not
stir just drain — add yolk
of 2 eggs — grated rind of
1 lemon — 2 cups milk
Put into dish and bake in
a moderate oven till done —
remove from oven and cool
Beat egg whites till stiff
add juice of lemon 3 cups
sugar spread this on top and
bake this slowly for about
¾ hr. try with silver
knife if clear it is done
Bake as a custard, this forms
sort of a jelly thro rice —

very good

Rinktum Tiddy (Gracie D)

1 pt. canned tomatoes
1 t. salt
1 t. sugar
1/8 t. pepper
D. C ...
1 T. chopped onion
1/2 lb. Cheese
1 t. butter
1 egg.

Buttered toast or crackers

Heat the tomatoes and add all seasonings. When hot melt in it the cheese cut in bits adding gradually while stirring constantly when smooth add the butter and egg beaten stirring all the while.

Rinktum Tiddy

❧

1 pint canned tomatoes
1 teaspoon salt
1 teaspoon sugar
⅛ teaspoon pepper
D.C. [dash cayenne pepper]
1 tablespoon chopped onion
½ pound cheese
1 teaspoon butter
1 egg
buttered toast or crackers

Heat the tomatoes and add all seasonings. When hot, melt in it the cheese, cut in bits, adding gradually while stirring constantly. When smooth, add the butter and egg, beaten, stirring all the while.

Tomatoe Bisque (Mrs Myers)

3 pts boiling milk
1 qt .. tomatoes

Add to the boiling milk
3 to. butter mixed with
2 J. cornstarch. add to the
boiling tomatoes 1 t. soda
strain tomatoes & pour in
boiling milk
season with salt & C. pepper
to taste
serve directly after putting
milk and tomatoe together

TOMATO BISQUE

❧

3 pints boiling milk
1 quart boiling tomatoes
3 teaspoons butter
2 tablespoons cornstarch
1 teaspoon baking soda
salt and pepper to taste

Add to the boiling milk butter, mixed with cornstarch.

Add to the boiling tomatoes soda. Strain tomatoes and pour in boiling milk. Season with salt and pepper to taste.

Serve directly after putting milk and tomatoes together.

Found in *Good Housekeeping Cook Book* by Dorothy B. Marsh.
Published by Good Housekeeping Book Division, 1962.

MACARONI LOAF

❧

1 package Royal gelatin (lemon)
1 cup boiling water
½ cup cold water
½ teaspoon salt
1½ tablespoons prepared mustard
3 tablespoons vinegar
⅔ cup mayonnaise
1 cup cooked elbow macaroni
⅔ cup chopped cabbage
2 tablespoons minced pimiento

Dissolve gel in boiling water. Add cold water, seasonings, and vinegar. Chill until it begins to thicken, then beat in mayonnaise.

Add remaining ingredients and mold in loaf pan. Chill until firm. Slice and serve as a salad or use as a sandwich filling.

If desired, add a few drops of Worcestershire sauce or onion juice and 2 minced green peppers.

Serves 8. Cost: 34 cents.

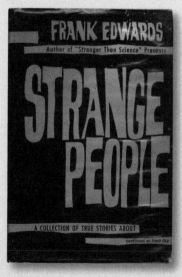

Found in *Strange People* by Frank Edwards.
Published by Lyle Stuart, 1961.

Macaroni Loaf

1 package Royal Gel. (Lemon.) Pud.
1 c boiling water
½ c cold water
½ t salt
1½ T prepared mustard
3 T vinegar
⅔ c mayonnaise
1 c cooked elbow macaroni
⅔ c chopped cabbage
2 T minced pimienta

Dissolve Gel in boiling H₂O, add cold H₂O, seasonings & vinegar. Chill until it begins to thicken, then beat in mayonnaise. Add remaining ingredients & mould in loaf pan chill until firm Slice & serve as a salad or use as a sandwich filling.

If desired add a few drops of Worcestershire Sauce or onion juice & 2 T minced green pepper.

Serves 8   Cost. 34¢
(F.B.Sauer)

Noodle Pudding   Sandra's

3/4 lb. Broad Egg Noodles
1 lb. Small Curd Cottage Cheese
1/4 lb. Veloceta Cheese - cut up
1 cup sour cream
1/4 c. sugar
1/4 lb Melted Butter

Cook Noodles (10 min) mix together
with above ingredients - Pour into
9 X 13 greased Pyrex Dish

              Second Mixture
4 eggs mix & beat with
1/2 cup sugar
1 3/4 cups milk
1 tsp. vanilla

Pour over first mixture - Coat
heavily with cinammon & sugar

        Bake 1 1/4 hrs at 350°
One half of above Recipe
        Serves about 6

Found in *The Wild, Unwilling Wife* by
Barbara Cartland. Published by
Bantam, 1978.

NOODLE PUDDING

❧

¾ pound broad egg noodles

1 pound small-curd cottage cheese

¼ pound Velveeta cheese, cut up

1 cup sour cream

¾ cup sugar, divided, plus some for topping

¼ cup melted butter

4 eggs

1 ¾ cups milk

1 teaspoon vanilla

cinnamon

Cook noodles for 10 minutes. Mix with cottage cheese, Velveeta, sour cream, ¼ cup sugar, and butter. Pour into 9-by-13-inch greased Pyrex dish.

Beat eggs, ½ cup sugar, milk and vanilla together. Pour over noodles. Coat heavily with cinnamon and sugar.

Bake for 1¼ hours at 350F. Half of the above recipe serves about 6.

Potato Soup

5 cups potatoes
½ cup celery, diced
⅓ cup onion, diced
salt, to taste
2 quarts water
white pepper, to taste
1 cup skim milk powder
1 cup cold water
chopped parsley, for garnish

In a heavy, 6-quart saucepan, place potatoes, celery, onion, salt, and water. Place over medium heat and bring to a boil.

Turn heat down to low and simmer for 40 to 50 minutes, or until vegetables are tender. Season with a few grindings of fresh pepper and additional salt.

Combine skim milk powder with cold water using a wire whisk. Stir into soup mixture and simmer over low heat for about 5 minutes, stirring constantly.

Ladle soup into tureen or individual soup bowls. Garnish with finely chopped parsley.

Makes 8 cups.

Found in *The Red Badge of Courage* by Stephen Crane. Published by Dover, 1990.

potatoe soup

5 cups potatoes

1/2 c celery diced

1/3 c onion diced

salt to taste

2 quarts water

white pepper to taste

1 c skim milk powder

1 c cold water

chopped parsley for garnish

① in heavy 6 quart sauce pan place dice potatoes, celery onion, salt, and water. place over medium heat and bring to boil turn heat down to low and simmer for 40 to 50 minutes or until vegetables are tender.

② season with few grindings of fresh pepper and additional salt

③ combine skim milk powder with one cup water using a wire wisk stir into soup mixture and

simmer over low heat for about 5 min stirring constantly.

④ ladle the soup into tureen or individual soup bowls. Garnish with finely chopped parsley. Makes 8 cups.

Okra Gumbo (Mama T's)

1/2 lb. bacon
1/2 " ham
2 " lean veal
1 large onion
3 lbs. tomatoes or 1 qt can
4 " okra or 1 small can
if canned ones use & drain
any raw boiling over then
the drain.
1/2 teasp. salt
1/8 " pepper
Slice bacon & cut in small
pieces, fry add ham & veal
cut in fine pieces add
onion chopped cook 10 min.
cover with tomatoes and
okra cut small cover and
cook gently 3 hrs. serve hot
on mashroom.

Okra Gumbo

½ pound bacon

½ pound ham

2 pounds lean veal

1 large onion

3 pounds tomatoes or 1 quart can

4 pounds okra or 1 small can (if canned ones used, drain and pour boiling over
them and drain)

½ teaspoon salt

⅛ teaspoon pepper

Slice bacon and cut in small pieces and fry. Add ham and veal, cut in fine pieces. Add onion, chopped; cook 10 minutes. Cover with tomatoes and okra, cut small. Cover and cook gently, 2 hours. Serve hot over rice or macaroni.

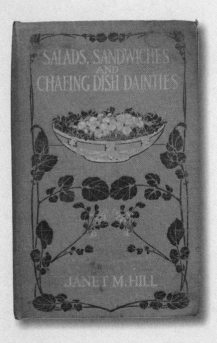

Found in *Salads, Sandwiches and Chafing Dish Dainties* by Janet M. Hill. Published by Little, Brown and Co., 1914.

SACCHARINE PICKLES

❧

1 tablespoon alum
2 tablespoons mustard seed
2 tablespoons mixed spices
2 teaspoons saccharine
⅔ cup salt
1 gallon vinegar

Heat together. Let cool before putting on pickles.

KOSHER DILL PICKLES

❧

20–25 dill size cucumbers
⅛ teaspoon powdered alum
1 clove garlic
2 heads dill
1 red hot pepper (if wanted)
1 quart vinegar
3 quarts water
1 cup salt

Wash cucumbers, let stand in ice water one night. Pack in sterile jars.

To each quart, add alum, garlic, dill. Combine vinegar, salt and water, and bring to a boil. Fill jars. Place dill in bottom.

Found in *The Spy Who Loved Me* by Ian Fleming.
Published by New American Library, 1963.

Sachrine Pickles
1 tablespoon alum
2 " mustard seed
2 " mixed spices
2 teasp. sachrine
2/3 cup salt
1 gal vinegar
Heat together. Let cool
before putting on pickles.

Kosher Dill Pickles
20-25 Dill size cucs.
1/8 teas powdered alum
1 clove garlic
2 heads dill
1 red hot pepper (if wanted)
1 qt vinegar-3 qts-water
1 cup salt
Wash cucs, let stand in
icewater one night & Pack
in sterile jars.
To each qt add alum garlic
dill. Combine vinegar,
salt & water & bring to boil
Fill jars place dill in bottom.

Found in *The Human Figure*
by J. H. Vanderpoel.
Published by the Inland
Printer Co., 1916.

Main Dishes

Barbecued Beef

❧

1 ½ pounds round steak, cut ¾ inch thick
½ teaspoon salt
¼ teaspoon paprika
⅓ cup flour
1 cup water
1 cup tomatoes
2 teaspoons chopped onion
4 tablespoons chili sauce

Wipe off the steak with a damp cloth. Cut into 2-inch pieces and pound. Sprinkle with salt, paprika and flour.

Brown in the fat which has been heated in frying pan. Add rest of ingredients and lid. Bake slow for 2 hours. Unmold and surround with sauce. Cut and serve hot.

Piquant Sauce

3 tablespoons butter
3 tablespoons flour
⅓ teaspoon paprika
1 ½ cups milk
1 egg
2 tablespoons finely cut sweet pickle

Mix butter, flour, salt, and paprika. Add milk. Cook until creamy sauce forms. Add rest of ingredients; cook for 1 minute, stirring constantly. Pour around loaf. Garnish with parsley. Serve hot. Serves 6.

Barbecued Beef, serving six—

1½ # round steak ⅔ in. thick—
½ tsp salt. ¼ tsp paprika. ⅓ cup flour
1 cup water - 1 cup tomatos
2 tsp chopped onion, 4 tbs chili sauce

Wipe off the steak with a damp
cloth. Cut into 2 in. pieces, pound
sprinkle with salt - paprika and
flour. Brown in the fat which
has been heated in frying pans add
rest of ingredients and lid. Bake slow
2 hr—

surround with
sauce cut and serve hot.

Piquant Sauce—
3 tbs butter— 3 tbs flour. ⅛ tsp paprika
1½ cups milk— 1 egg. 2 tbs finely cut
pimentors. 2 tbs finely cut sweet pickle
mix butter and flour salt paprika
add milk—cook till creamy sauce
forms. add rest of ingredients cook
1 min. stirring constantly pour around
loaf garnish with parsley—Serve hot—

Found in *Meat Handbook of the United States Navy* (no author). Published by the U.S. Government Printing Office, 1945.

Chef Meat Sauce

1 cup mayonnaise
⅓ cup chili sauce
¾ cup mustard
¼ cup onion, shredded
1 tablespoon horseradish
1 teaspoon oregano
⅛ teaspoon cayenne pepper
⅓ cup sour cream

Mix first seven ingredients. Strain chili sauce to remove seeds. Beat in with a fork. Blend in sour cream. Let stand for 2 days in refrigerator. Use on meat, fish or poultry.

Found in *Marjorie at Seacote* by Carolyn Wells. Published by Grosset & Dunlap, 1912.

HAM 'N' LAMB KABOBS

Note: This recipe suggests that these kabobs should be served with pineapple fritters, but does not include instructions for that part of the dish.

3 pounds lamb shoulder, cut in 1½-inch squares,
¾ inch thick (allow 3 pieces per skewer)
salt and pepper
1½ pounds smoked ham slice, cut into 1-inch squares,
⅜ inch thick, 2 pieces to a skewer
butter

Season lamb with salt and pepper. Slip lamb and ham alternately on skewers. Brush with melted butter. Broil 6 inches from heat, 20–25 minutes. Use preheated broiler. Makes 12 kabobs.

ADDITIONAL KABOBS

1. Cubes of cooked ham and orange or pineapple.

2. Frankfurters cut in 1-inch cubes, spread with mustard, with tomato quarters.

Found in *The Joy of Chinese Cooking* by Doreen Yen Hung Fen. Published by Greenberg (no date; circa 1950s).

Ham 'n' Lamb Kabobs
on pineapple fritters
3 lbs lamb shoulder cut
in 1½" squares ¾" thick allow
3 pieces to a skewer
Salt & pepper

1½ lbs smoked ham slice
cut in 1" sq. ³⁄₁₆" thick 2 pieces
to a skewer.

Butter
Season lamb with salt, pepper
slip alternately on skewers
brush with melted butter broil
6 in. from heat 20-25 min
12 Kabobs use preheated broiler
Additional Kabobs
1. Cubes of cooked ham and orange & pineapple
2. Frankfurters cut in 1 in. cubes spread
with mustard with tomatoe quarters.

Stuffed peppers.
4 peppers
1½ cups cooked macaroni.
1 can mushroom soup
grated cheese 4 tbl.
Onion 1 tbl.
Parsley 4 tbl.
Ham 2 cup

Mix macaroni onion parsley
and meat.
Sprinkle top with cheese.
Bake in oven 375° for 15 min.

Found in *The ABC of Casseroles*
(no author). Published by Peter
Pauper Press, 1954.

Stuffed Peppers

❧

4 peppers

1 ½ cups cooked macaroni

1 can mushroom soup

4 tablespoons grated cheese

1 tablespoon onion

1 tablespoon parsley

½ cup ham

Mix soup, macaroni, onion, parsley, and meat. Sprinkle top with cheese.

Bake in oven at 375 degrees for 15 minutes.

(Italian pie)

1 lb. butts - ground or cut up
in small pieces.
1 leg of pepperoni sausage
1 package of provolone — 2 lb. or
cheese   more
1 large or 2 medium onions
parsley
grated cheese
4 or more eggs

Fry butts nice & brown,
add onions & fry with
butts until tender - add
salt & pepper

Grind pepperoni & cheese
in food chopper & put in
large bowl. Add butts &
onions. Add parsley, grated
cheese & eggs & mix all
to-gether.

Make crust like pie crust
add egg yolk & milk
instead of water.

Bake like pie until
done

Found in *The Talisman Italian Cook
Book* by Ada Boni. Published by
Crown Publishers, 1955.

THE TALISMAN
Italian Cook Book

Italian Pie

1 pound butts, ground or cut up in small pieces
1 leg of pepperoni sausage
1 package of provolone cheese (½ pound or more)
1 large or 2 medium onions
parsley
grated cheese
4 or more eggs

Fry butts nice and brown. Add onions and fry with butts until tender. Add salt and pepper.

Grind pepperoni and cheese in food chopper and put in large bowl. Add fried butts and onions. Add parsley, grated cheese, and eggs; mix all together.

Make crust like piecrust. Add egg yolk and milk instead of water.

Bake like pie until done.

As I have mentioned before, I'm no cook, but the few dishes I do enjoy making are firmly Italian in origin. One of those dishes is a calzone, which is why the next recipe intrigued me. Italian Pie looked to be similar, with the notable difference being the piecrust instead of the traditional pizza crust.

I sent this recipe along to Tammy Cannon at *Speckle of Dirt* (http://speckleofdirt.com) for some insight. She describes her site as "a blog about how food inspires us to be a better person. Food sparks memories, eliminates boundaries, encourages creativity, and is timeless." Tammy has tested recipes for my blog before, and I thought she would find out if Italian Pie was a keeper.

When Michael sent over the recipe for Italian Pie, I was a bit nervous. I thought I might be in trouble when I read the words "1 pound butts, ground" and "leg of pepperoni sausage" because these aren't words I typically use in cooking. Then there was the phrase "make crust like piecrust" and "bake like pie until done," and I grew even more nervous. I would have to create this recipe almost from scratch, while honoring the original intent of the writer. Here is my version of this wonderful Italian Pie. This dish held together well, lending itself to being eaten like a pizza. Perfect for a picnic. Thank you, stranger. You gave my family a new favorite dish.

I used a buttered 10½-inch false bottom tart pan for this dish. You could use a pie dish, but the size of this pan went perfectly with the amount of crust yielded by the pastry. I baked this dish in a 350-degree oven for approximately 55 minutes. I started at 30, and then increased it in 10-minute increments, until the final 5. You might bake it faster at 375 for 45 minutes.

FILLING (MODIFIED)
1 pound ground beef
1 (8-ounce) package of pepperoni
1½ pounds provolone cheese
1 large onion, diced
1 handful of parsley, chopped
½ cup grated Parmesan cheese
4 eggs

PIECRUST (MODIFIED)
1¼ cups flour
2 tablespoons olive oil
1 pinch salt
⅔ cup warm water

Mix the flour and salt together in a mixing bowl, and add the oil. Knead for 5 minutes on a lightly floured surface. Set aside while you make the filling.

Brown the ground beef in a skillet, stirring often to prevent too much browning. Add the onions and cook until the onions are translucent and meat is fully cooked. Add salt and pepper to taste. Set aside in a large mixing bowl.

In a food processor, add pepperoni and provolone cheese. and pulse until chopped into little pieces. Add to the browned beef and onions.

Now that the beef and pepperoni mixture are in the mixing bowl, add parsley, grated Parmesan cheese, and the eggs. Mix until everything is well incorporated using a mixing spoon.

To ASSEMBLE: Take the pastry dough that has been resting, and cut it in half with a knife or pastry cutter.

Roll out into a large disk about 10½ inches in diameter, and press into a prepared pie tin with scalloped edge and false bottom. Make sure to press the dough against the scalloped edge.

Add the filling to the pie tin on top of the pastry.

Roll out the other half of the pastry dough, and gently place it on top of the filling, making sure to press it against the sides of the tin to reveal a nice edge when the pie is all finished.

Make small decorative slices on top of the pastry dough.

Bake for 55 minutes in a 350-degree oven. Remove from oven and let cool for 10 minutes. Remove the false bottom and cut into eight slices.

TAMMY CANNON

Meat & Cheese Loaf

2 lbs ground round steak
1½ cup cubed cheese
2 eggs
1 onion chopped
1 green pepper
2 t. salt
1 t pepper
1 t celery salt
½ t. paprika
1½ cup evaporated milk
1½ .. water
1 .. dry bread crumbs

bake 1½ hours. serve 10-12

MEAT AND CHEESE LOAF

2 pounds ground round steak

1½ cups cubed cheese

2 eggs

1 onion, chopped

1 green pepper

2 teaspoons salt

1 teaspoon pepper

1 teaspoon celery salt

½ teaspoon paprika

1½ cups evaporated milk

1½ cups water

1½ cups dry bread crumbs

Combine all ingredients. Bake for 1½ hours. Serves 10 to 12.

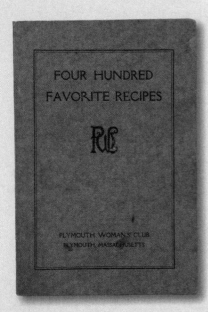

FOUR HUNDRED
FAVORITE RECIPES

RC

PLYMOUTH WOMAN'S CLUB
PLYMOUTH, MASSACHUSETTS

Found in *Four Hundred Favorite Recipes* by the Plymouth Women's Club. Published by the Memorial Press, 1929.

Lamb Loaf

❧

2 cups chopped lamb
1 cup bread crumbs
2 egg yolks, or 1 egg
2 tablespoons chopped onion
2 tablespoons chopped celery
2 cups milk
2 tablespoons chopped pimiento
2 tablespoons gravy or butter

SAVORY SAUCE
3 tablespoons butter
4 tablespoons flour
1⅔ cups milk
2 tablespoons chopped olives
1 tablespoon chopped parsley
2 tablespoons chopped green pepper

Mix loaf ingredients together and put in loaf pan. Bake 30 minutes.

Combine sauce ingredients and cook until a cream sauce forms. Serve around the lamb loaf.

Lamb Loaf.

2 cups chopped lamb.
1 "   bread crumbs. 2 egg yolks or 1 egg
1 tbs chopped onions.
2 "   "   celery. 3 cups milk.
2 "   "   pimento. 2 tbs. gravy or butter.
Mix ingredients, put into loaf pan
bake 30 min.
          Serve with savory sauce.
3 tbs butter. 4 tbs. flour. 1½ cups milk.
2 " chopped olives. 1 tbs chopped parsley
2 " green pepper. cook till a cream sauce
forms, serve around the lamb loaf.

Found in *The Picnic Book* by
Clark L. Fredrickson. Published
by A. S. Barnes and Co., 1942.

MEAT BALL MEXICANA

I pound ground beef   4 Tablespoons shorting

½ cup rolled oats   I NO. 2 can tomatoes

INo. 2 can tomatojuice   I bay leaf

3/4 cup chopped onions   I teasooon chilli powder

2½ teaspoonssalt   I package frozen mixed vegetables

Iteaspoon Worcester sauce   ½ cup washed macaroni

Mildred

MEAT BALL MEXICANA

❧

1 pound ground beef
½ cup rolled oats
1 No. 2 can tomato juice
¾ cup chopped onions
2½ teaspoons salt
1 teaspoon Worcestershire sauce
4 tablespoons shortening
1 No. 2 can tomatoes
1 bay leaf
1 teaspoon chili powder
1 package frozen vegetables
½ cup washed macaroni

Found in *The Carbondale Cookbook* by the
Young Lady Workers of the Methodist
Episcopal Church of Carbondale,
Pennsylvania. Publisher and date unknown.

Sweet and Sour Pork

½ pound lean pork
dry white wine
¼ teaspoon each salt and pepper
½ cup pineapple chunks
1 green pepper, cut into 1-inch squares
½ cup chopped carrot

BATTER

½ cup flour
¼ cup cornstarch
½ teaspoon baking powder
1 tablespoon beaten egg
½ cup water less ½ tablespoon
1 teaspoon oil

SAUCE

¾ cup sugar
⅓ cup ketchup
1 tablespoon soy sauce
¼ teaspoon salt
½ cup white vinegar
¼ teaspoon MSG
⅔ cup plus ½ cup water
3½ tablespoons cornstarch
1 tablespoon oil

Cut pork into bite-size chunks. Marinate in white wine, seasoned with salt and pepper. Prepare pineapple, pepper, and carrot.

Combine batter ingredients. Coat pork in batter and deep-fry to light brown color.

Combine cornstarch, oil, and ½ cup water. Mix with remaining sauce ingredients and cook together.

Parboil carrots and pepper, carrots for 1 minute and pepper momentarily.

Add vegetables and pineapple to sauce after pork has been deep-fried for a second time to a golden-brown color. Pour sauce over meat, which has been placed on a platter.

SWEET AND SOUR PORK

Cut ½ lb. of lean pork in bite sized chunks
Marinate ½ hour in dry white wine with ¼tsp.salt and pepper.
Also make ready ½ cup chunk pineapple, one green pepper
   cut in 1 inch squares and ½ cup cut up carrot.

BATTER FOR PORK
½ cup flour
¼ cup corn starch
½ tsp. baking powder
1 tbs. beaten egg
½ cup water less ½tbs.
1 tsp. oil
   Coat pork chunks with batter and deep fry to light
   brown color.

SWEET AND SOUR SAUCE
3/4 cup sugar
1/3 cup catsup
1 tbs. Soy sauce
¼ tsp. salt
½ cup white vinsgar
¼ tsp. MSG
2/3 cup water
3½ tbs. corn starch) together
1/2 cup water   )
1 tbs. oil
   Mix ingredients and cook together.
   Parboil carrots and pepper, carrots for 1 minute
   and pepper momentarily.
   Add to sweet and sour sauce after pork chunks
   have been dreep frieid for a second time to a
   golden brown color. Pour over meat chunks which
   have been placed on a platter.

Whitney R. Cross **The Burned-Over District**
The Social and Intellectual History
of Enthusiastic Religion in
Western New York, 1800-1850

HARPER TORCHBOOKS

Found in *The Burned-Over District* by Whitney R. Cross. Published by Harper Torchbooks, 1965.

chicken legs

1/4 cup oil   Bake 55 min.
1 (8 oz) crushed pineapple
                   drained.
1/4 cup Lemon juice
1/4 cup Karo syrup
2 tbl soy sauce
1 tsp salt
1/4 pepper
1/4 Ginger

Combine oil, pineapple juice, syrup
soy sauce, salt, pepper, ginger
Put chicken in baking dish. Bake 375°

Chicken Legs

½ cup oil

1 (8.5-ounce) can crushed pineapple, drained

¼ cup lemon juice

¼ cup Karo syrup

2 tablespoons soy sauce

1 teaspoon salt

¼ teaspoon pepper

¼ teaspoon ginger

Combine oil, pineapple, lemon juice, syrup, soy sauce, salt, pepper, and ginger. Put chicken in baking dish and cover in sauce. Bake at 375 for 55 minutes.

Found in *Catch-22* by Joseph Heller. Published by Dell, 1965.

SCALLOPED SALMON
WITH NOODLES AND ALMONDS

¼ pound egg noodles (1 cup cooked)
1 cup flaked salmon
½ cup chopped almonds
salt and pepper
2 cups white sauce (recipe follows)

Cook noodles until soft in 1½ quarts boiling water, salted.

Combine with nuts, salmon, salt and pepper. Pour over this white sauce. Top with bread crumbs or Wheaties. Bake 20 minutes.

WHITE SAUCE

4 tablespoons butter
4 tablespoons flour
salt and pepper
2 cups milk

Blend and boil for 2 minutes.

Found in *A Book for a Cook* by L. P. Hubbard.
Published by Pillsbury, 1905.

Scalloped Salmon
with noodles & Almonds

1/4 lb. egg noodles (1 cup uncooked)
1 cup flaked salmon
1/2 " Chopped Almonds
Salt & pepper
2 cups white sauce
cook noodles until soft in
1 1/2 qt. Boiling water salted.
Combine with nuts, salmon Salt
& pepper, pour over this white
sauce top with bread crumbs
or wheaties bake 20 min.

White sauce
4 Tablsp. butter
4 " flour
Salt & pepper   blend &
2 cups milk   boil 2 min.

Tuna Croquettes

mix 35 Ritz Crackers
(on 1 stack pack) crushed
with 7 g. can tuna,
drained, flaked;
1/4 c milk, 1/2 tsp basil,
1/8 tsp pepper,
1 Beaten egg & chill

Shape each croquette around

1-inch cub american cheese.
Roll in Ritz crumbs.
Saute in 1/4 inch
hot fat until well
Browned. Makes 6-8
croquettes

Tuna Croquettes

35 Ritz crackers (1 stack pack), crushed
1 (7-ounce) can tuna, drained and flaked
¼ cup milk
½ teaspoon basil
⅛ teaspoon pepper
1 egg, beaten
American cheese, cut into 1-inch cubes

Mix together all ingredients except cheese, reserving some cracker crumbs, and chill. Shape each croquette around a cube of cheese. Roll in remaining cracker crumbs. Sauté in ½ inch of hot fat until well browned. Makes 6 to 8 croquettes.

Found in *Gateway to the Great Books, vol. 10: Philosophical Essays* edited by Robert M. Hutchins and Mortimer J. Adler. Published by Encyclopedia Britannica, 1963.

CHICKEN AND SPAGHETTI CASSEROLE

2 cups cooked chopped chicken

1½ cup chicken broth

2 cups broken spaghetti, uncooked

½ cup diced celery

½ cup diced onion

¼ cup diced green pepper

1 cup cream of mushroom soup

1½ cup grated cheese (reserve ¾ cup for topping)

Cook spaghetti and mix all together. Put in greased casserole.

Cover with foil. Bake 1 hour, 350 degrees.

Sprinkle ¾ cup cheese on top. Bake 15 minutes longer.

Found in *Sphere* by Michael Crichton.
Published by Alfred A. Knopf, 1987.

Chick Spaghetti cass.

2 C cooked chopped chick.
1½ C chic. broth
2 C broken spaghetti uncooked
1½ C diced celery
½ " onion
¼ " G pepper

1 C cream mushroom soup
1½ C grated cheese reserve
Cover with foil.   ¾ C for top.
Cook spaghetti + mix all
together put in greased casserole
Sprinkle ¾ C cheese on top bake
15 min longer

Bake 1 hr 350°

Spagetti Sauce
5 C tomatoes (in Ble...
1 12 oz tomato paste
1 tbs sugar
1 ½ tsp salt
½ tsp pepper
1 ½ tsp ~~sugar~~ orgaeno
¾ C onion
Cook 1 hr to 1 ½ hr
put in Canner 10 min

35 c tomatoes
7 cans paste
7 tbl sugar
10 ½ tsp salt
3 ½ tsp pepper
10 ½ tsp. El regano
2 c onions
Cook down about 4 hrs.

Spaghetti Sauce

⌘

5 cups tomatoes (in blender)
1 (12-ounce) can tomato paste
1 tablespoon sugar
1 ½ teaspoons salt
½ teaspoon pepper
1 ½ teaspoons oregano
¾ cup onion

Cook 1 to 1½ hours. Put in canner for 10 minutes.

Large-Scale Recipe

35 cups tomatoes
7 cans paste
7 tablespoons sugar
10 ½ teaspoons salt
3 ½ teaspoons pepper
10 ½ teaspoons oregano
2 cups onions

Cook down about 4 hours.

Found in *The New Art of Modern Cooking*
by the General Electric Kitchen
Institute. Published by General
Electric, 1937.

Red Pepper Quiche

1 (9-inch) piecrust, partially baked (15 minutes) in quiche plate
1 onion, thinly sliced
4 tablespoons oleo
2 red sweet peppers, diced
1½ pounds good sharp cheddar or Gruyère cheese
4 eggs
½ pint heavy cream or evaporated milk
½ cup milk
¼ teaspoon cayenne pepper
1 teaspoon salt
sprinkling of parsley and thyme

Sauté onion; set aside. Heat 2 tablespoons oleo. Add peppers. Sauté quickly. Fill crust with peppers, onions, cream, and cheese. Whip eggs and milk. Pour over pepper mixture.

Bake at 350 degrees for 45 minutes. Test with knife—if knife is clean, it's done.

Serve this with a lusty green salad, and you'll have happy palates.

Found in *It Came from Schenectady* by Barry B. Longyear. Published by Popular Library, 1986.

Red Pepper Quiche

1 9-in. pie crust, partially baked (15 min) in quiche plate.
1 onion, thinly sliced
4 T oleo
2 red sweet peppers, diced
1½ lb. good sharp chedder cheese or Gruy.
5 eggs
½ pt Heavy Cr (I use Evap
½ C milk
¼ tsp cayenne

tsp. salt
sprinkling of parsley and thyme
Sauté onion, set aside. Heat 2 T oleo. Add peppers. Sauté quickly. Fill crust with peppers, onions, cream an cheese. Whip eggs and milk. Pour over pepper mixture Bake 350° 45 min. Test with Knife — if Knife is clean, it's done.

Serve this with a lusty green salad and you'll have happy palates.

Pasta with Artichokes, capers & Tomatoes

2 T. onions chopped	3 T. fresh Parsley minced
2 T. minced garlic	3/4 C. chicken Broth
2 T. olive oil	1/3 C. Sour cream
28 g can Plum Tomatoes	1 C. Half & Half
6 oz chopped marinated Artichoke hearts	1 t. Each Basil & Oregano
	1/2 t. ground coriander
3 T. capers drained	

Cook onion & garlic in olive oil 'til softened
Add tomatoes & juice – Simmer 5 min.
  " Artichokes & capers & " " "
  " Herbs & Broth – Bring to Boil & Boil 5 m
  " Sour cream & half & half – Simmer 10 –
      until slightly thickened –
Serve over capellini (verythin spaghetti) or
  pasta – Parmeson to taste

Found in *Dune: Messiah* by Frank Herbert.
Published by G. P Putnam, 1969.

PASTA WITH ARTICHOKES, CAPERS, AND TOMATOES

⤞

2 tablespoons onions, chopped

2 tablespoons minced garlic

2 tablespoons olive oil

1 (25-ounce) can plum tomatoes

6 ounces chopped marinated artichoke hearts

3 tablespoons capers, drained

3 tablespoons fresh parsley, minced

¾ cup chicken broth

⅓ cup sour cream

1 cup half-and-half

1 teaspoon each basil and oregano

½ teaspoon ground coriander

Cook onion and garlic in olive oil until softened.

Add tomatoes with juice; simmer for 5 minutes. Add artichokes and capers; simmer for another 5 minutes. Add herbs and broth; bring to a boil and boil for 5 minutes. Add sour cream and half-and-half; simmer for 10 to 15 minutes, or until slightly thickened.

Serve over cappellini (very thin spaghetti) or other pasta. Add Parmesan to taste.

RECEIPT FOR ONE CASE OF
STRAWBERRIES, PURCHASED FROM THE
W. H. STEVENS COMPANY OF SEAFORD,
DELAWARE, DATED JUNE 4, 1890

Found in *The Regent's Daughter* by
Alexandre Dumas. Published by Little,
Brown and Co., 1904.

Desserts

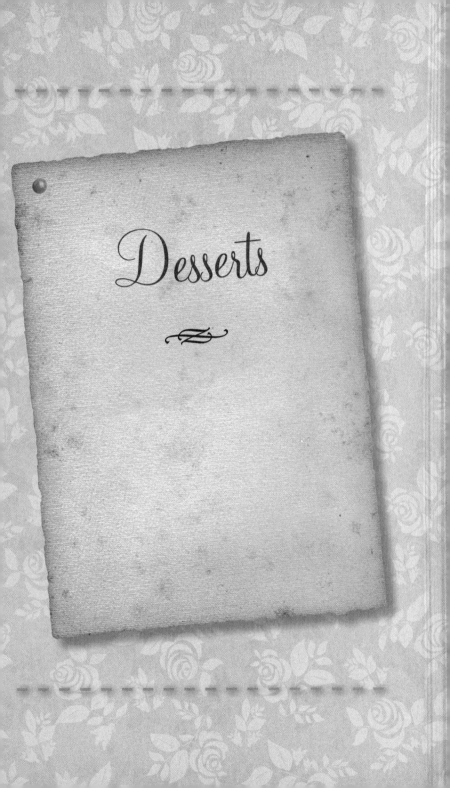

BLONDE BROWNIES

2 cups flour
1 teaspoon baking powder
2 cups packed brown sugar
2 eggs
1 cup chocolate chips
¼ teaspoon baking soda
1 teaspoon salt
⅔ cup shortening, melted
2 teaspoons vanilla
⅓ cup chopped nuts

Mix flour, baking soda, baking powder, and salt. Add sugar to shortening, along with eggs and vanilla. Add flour mixture to sugar mixture. Spread in 13-by-9-inch pan. Sprinkle with chips and nuts. Bake at 350 for 30 minutes. Cool in pan; cut bars.

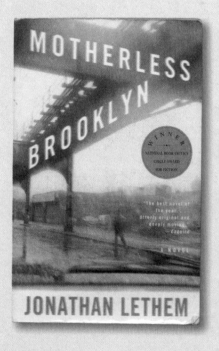

Found in *Motherless Brooklyn* by Jonathan Lethem. Published by Vintage Books, 1999.

Blonde Brownies

c. flour   4 teas. Baking Soda
teas Baking powder   1 teas salt
packed Brown Sugar   2/3 c. shortening melted
eggs   2 teas Vanilla
c. Choc chips   1/3 c. chopped nuts

Mix flour, Soda Baking powder + salt
add Sugar to shortening - eggs - vanilla
add flour mixture to sugar mixture
Spread in 13 x 9 pan. Sprinkle with chips +
nuts
Bake 350° for 30 min.
Cool in pan; cut in bars.

350°

Paul's Pumpkin Bars

4 - eggs
1⅔ - cups sugar
1 - cup oil
1 - 16 oz can pumpkin
2 - cups flour
2 - tsp. baking powder
2 - tsp. ground cinnamon
1 - tsp. salt
1 - tsp. baking soda

1 - 3 oz cream cheese - softened
½ - cup butter or oleo softened
1 - tsp. vanilla
2 - cups sifted powdered sugar

In mixer bowl, beat together
eggs, sugar, oil and pumpkin till
light and fluffy. Stir together
flour, baking powder, cinnamon
salt and soda. Add to pumpkin
mixture and mix thoroughly.
        Spread batter in ungreas
15 × 10 × 1 in baking pan.
    Bake 350° 25-30 min.
Cool and frost.

        Cream cheese Icing

    Cream together cream cheese
and butter or oleo.
        Stir in vanilla, add
powdered sugar, a little at a
time, beating well, till
mixture is smooth

PAUL'S PUMPKIN BARS

❧

4 eggs

1⅔ cups sugar

1 cup oil

1 (16-ounce) can pumpkin

2 cups flour

2 teaspoons baking powder

2 teaspoons ground cinnamon

1 teaspoon salt

1 teaspoon baking soda

3 ounces cream cheese, softened

½ cup butter or oleo, softened

1 teaspoon vanilla

2 cups sifted powdered sugar

In mixer bowl, beat together eggs, sugar, oil, and pumpkin until light and fluffy. In a separate bowl, stir together flour, baking powder, cinnamon, salt, and baking soda. Add to pumpkin mixture, mixing thoroughly.

Spread batter in an ungreased 15-by-10-by-1-inch baking pan. Bake at 350 degrees for 25 to 30 minutes. Cool and frost (recipe follows).

CREAM CHEESE ICING

Cream together cream cheese and butter or oleo. Stir in vanilla. Add powdered sugar, a little at a time, beating well, until mixture is smooth.

ALMOND CHRISTMAS BALLS

1 cup butter or oleo
¾ cup confectioner's sugar
2 cups sifted all-purpose flour
1 cup ground almonds (2 ounces)
1 teaspoon vanilla extract
18 candied cherries

Cream butter or oleo with sugar until fluffy. Add everything else except the cherries and mix well with your hands.

Take 1 teaspoon of dough and start to form into a ball. Push in a half cherry and roll again in your hands to make a perfect ball.

Makes about 3 dozen.

Bake on greased baking sheet in slow oven, 325F, 35 minutes.

While hot, roll in confectioner's sugar.

Dear Virginia,

If you'd like another receipt of another Christmas cookie I have one it's called Christmas Rocks, they are a harder cookie with mixed candied fruit and nuts. Well, let me know if you want it. Be seeing you.

The Bloomer Girl,
Mary C.

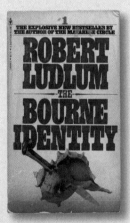

Found in *The Bourne Identity* by Robert Ludlum. Published by Bantam Books, 1980.

Almond Christmas Balls

1 c. butter, or oleo
3/4 c. Confectionery sugar
2 c. sifted all purpose flour
1 c. ground almonds (or 3)
1 tsp. vanilla extract
18 candied cherries

Cream butter or oleo with sugar until fluffy.
add everything else except the cherries and
mix well with your hands. Take one tsp.
of dough and start to form into a ball.
Push in a half cherry and roll again in
your hands to make a perfect ball.
(makes about 3 dozen.)
Bake on greased baking sheet in slow
oven. 325°F. 35 min.
While hot roll in confectionary sugar.

Dear Virginia,
   If you'd like another receipt of another
Christmas cookie, I have one it's called
Christmas Rocks. they are a harder
cookie with mixed candied fruit +
nuts. Well let me know if you
want it. Be seeing you.

                        The Bloomer girl,
                        Mary C.

Cherry Walnut Bars
(nice for holidays)

2¼ c. sifted flour
½ c. sugar
1 c. butter (softened)
2 eggs
1 c. brown sugar (firmly packed)
½ tsp. salt
½ tsp. baking powder
½ tsp. vanilla
1 (2 oz.) jar maraschino cherries
½ c. walnuts chopped
½ c. flaked coconut (optional)

Mix flour, sugar, & butter until crumbly. Press into 13x9x2 pan. Bake 350° in oven 20 min. or until crust is lightly brown. Blend eggs, sugar, salt, baking powder & vanilla. Drain & chop cherries reserving liquid. Stir chopped cherries and walnuts into egg-sugar mixture. Pour on top of baked crust. Return to oven & bake 25 min. Remove from oven & cool. Combine 1 tbsp. softened butter & 1 c. confectionary sugar with enough (over)

Cherry liquid to spread frost, sprinkle with coconut if you wish. When icing has set, cut into bars. Makes 4 doz.

Found in *9th Grand National Cook Book* by Ann Pillsbury.
Published by Pillsbury, 1958.

CHERRY WALNUT BARS

(Nice for holidays)

2¼ cups sifted flour
½ cup sugar
1 cup butter, softened
2 eggs
1 cup brown sugar, firmly packed
½ teaspoon salt
½ teaspoon baking powder
½ teaspoon vanilla
1 (2-ounce) jar maraschino cherries
½ cup walnuts, chopped
½ cup flaked coconut (optional)

FROSTING
1 tablespoon softened butter
1 cup confectioner's sugar
reserved liquid from maraschino cherries

Mix flour, sugar, and butter until crumbly. Press into 13-by-9-by-2-inch pan.

Bake at 350 degrees for 20 minutes or until crust is lightly brown.

Blend eggs, brown sugar, salt, baking powder, and vanilla. Drain and chop cherries, reserving liquid. Stir chopped cherries and walnuts into egg-sugar mixture.

Place on top of baked crust. Return to oven and bake for 25 minutes. Remove from oven and cool.

Combine frosting ingredients, adding enough cherry liquid to create a spreadable frosting. Frost bars and sprinkle with coconut, if desired. Cut into bars.

Makes 4 dozen.

Cloud Nine Butterscotch Bars

1 c. margarine	1 tsp. Baking powder
1 pkg Instant Butterscotch pudding	½ c. Milk
2 eggs	1 c. Quick oats (uncooked)
1 tsp. Vanilla	1 pkg (1 c.) choc. chips
1 c. flour	Choc. frosting.

Oven 350°. Beat Butter-pudding Mix - egg-vanilla
Sift flour + Baking powder - Milk. By hand stir in
oats - choc chips. Spread Batter in 9"
square Baking pan. Bake 20-25 min.
Cool - then spread with choc frosting - cut
in squares.

Found in *The Dairy Cookbook* by Olga Nickles. Published by Celestial Arts, 1976.

Cloud Nine Butterscotch Bars

∽

½ cup margarine
1 package instant butterscotch pudding
2 eggs
1 teaspoon vanilla
1 cup flour
1 teaspoon baking powder
½ cup milk
1 cup quick oats, uncooked
1 package (1 cup) chocolate chips
chocolate frosting

Preheat oven to 350 degrees.

Beat butterscotch pudding mix, eggs and vanilla.

Sift flour and baking powder. Combine wet and dry ingredients; add milk.

By hand, stir in oats and chocolate chips.

Spread batter in a 9-inch square baking pan. Bake for 20–25 minutes.

Cool, then spread with chocolate frosting. Cut into squares.

Maple Sugar

Heat Maple Syrup to 238° F
on candy thermometer
Cool slightly then stir syrup
Pack Mixture in mold or
leave in bowl and ~~crumble~~
sugar when it has cooled
completely.
Can be used sprinkled over
pancakes – pudding – Hot Rice.

New York to California on a
motor scooter with the author of
THE LAST UNICORN
PETER S. BEAGLE
05¢

**I SEE
BY MY
OUTFIT**

Found in *I See by My Outfit* by Peter S.
Beagle. Published by Ballantine, 1971.

Maple Sugar

~

Heat maple syrup to 238 degrees on candy thermometer.

Cool slightly then stir syrup.

Pack mixture in molds or leave in bowl and crumble sugar when it has cooled completely.

Can be used sprinkled over pancakes—pudding—hot rice.

Not long after I posted this recipe to my blog, a reader from Scotland sent me an email, insisting that she recognized both the book and the recipe:

> I was just killing some time randomly link-clicking when I stumbled across the recipe on your site. I looked at the book, first, and thought—hey, I remember that book! I remember it; I never read that particular copy of it, I just remember it from its home in a cabinet in the dining room, of all places. Then I looked at the recipe . . . looked at it again . . . looked at it again. That looked just like my mom's handwriting! Well, that was when I left the comment on your site.
>
> The book was either given away or lost when we moved house from Pennsylvania to Colorado in 1978. I was blown away when you were willing and able to send it to me. My mother is still alive, but her mind is not what it used to be; this brought back memories of when I was still very little and she was still very much my mom. It was such a strange, random little opportunity to revisit a small part of those years!
>
> I believe this recipe was given to her by her friend Ada around 1974. I remember how happy I was as a little girl to have the possibility of maple sugar on demand—I've always been greedy for that stuff. But when I started to make it . . . ha! That's when I remembered why we never ended up making it much.

The recipe calls for heating the maple syrup to 238 degrees F. If you don't, it won't crystallize when it cools. Unfortunately, when it goes a little over 200 degrees, it starts to boil, and when it gets to about 220 degrees, it is in full roiling boiling foaminess—and I had underestimated how deep the pot it was in needed to be! It foams up ferociously, and I was forced to drop the heat before it inundated the stove with cooking maple syrup!

I tried boiling it on lower temperature for a bit longer, but it's no use—it has to hit the right temperature, or it just remains quite stubbornly syrup.

Finally, I tried a very deep pot, usually used for large batches of chili. This was a wise decision; you would not believe how much that stuff actually foamed. I managed to get it to the prescribed temperature as well. But, as of this morning, it was rather disappointingly not quite sugar. It was no longer syrup, not really; it achieved a consistency rather like a semiliquid saltwater taffy. I don't remember that outcome when I was a little kid. However, I do think I know why we didn't use the recipe very often! Still tastes good, but it's a bit challenging to eat.

Lynne Batik

KOLOCKI

DOUGH
½ pound butter, softened
½ pound cream cheese, softened
4 egg yolks or 2 whole eggs
4 tablespoons sugar
2½ teaspoons baking powder
2¼ cups flour

FILLING
2 cups nuts, chopped
2–3 tablespoons sugar
hot water

Cream butter and cheese together. Add eggs.

Sift together sugar, baking powder and flour. Gradually add to creamed mixture. Refrigerate for 2 to 3 hours, or overnight.

Combine filling ingredients, adding enough hot water to form a paste.

Roll out dough thin and top with filling. Cut into squares, and roll up.

Bake at 425 degrees for 8 to 10 minutes. Sprinkle with confectioner's sugar.

Kolacki

1/4 lb butter   ) soft creamy
3/4 lb cream cheese)

4 egg yolks or 2 whole eggs
4 tablespoons sugar
3 1/2 teasp. B. powder   ) sift together
2 1/4 cups flour

Cream butter + cheese. Add eggs.
Add flour mixture gradually. Keep
in refrigerator over night or for 3
hrs. Roll out thin + (fp with
Nut filling (cut dough in squares, roll up)
    2 cups nuts chopped
2 or 3 tbl. sugar
Enough hot water to make a paste.
Bake 425° for 8 to 10 min.
Sprinkle with conf. sugar.

Found in *The Elements of Grammar* by
Margaret Shertzer. Published by Collier
Books, 1986.

Italian Cookies
11 eggs
1 lb sugar
1/2 lb. lard (melted)
3 lbs flour
15 - 1/2 tsp baking powder
salt
vanilla or lemon
flavoring
350° - 10 min.

ITALIAN COOKIES

~

11 eggs

1 pound sugar

½ pound lard, melted

3 pounds flour

15½ teaspoons baking powder

salt

vanilla or lemon flavoring

Combine all ingredients. Bake at 350 degrees for 10 minutes.

Found in *The Sun in Scorpio* by
Margery Sharp. Published by
Perennial Library, 1982.

MINCE MEAT COOKIES

3¼ cups sifted flour
½ teaspoon salt
1 teaspoon soda
1 cup shortening
1½ cups sugar
3 eggs, well beaten
1 package None Such Mince Meat

Sift flour, salt, and soda.

Cream shortening. Add sugar gradually.

Add eggs; beat until smooth.

Add mince meat, broken in small pieces. Add flour and mix well.

Drop by tablespoonfuls on greased baking sheet. Bake in oven 400 degrees, 12 minutes.

Found in *Favorite Recipes of Famous Chefs* by Emma C. Caron. Published by Robert McBride & Co., 1927.

Mince Meat Cookies

3¼ cups sifted flour
½ teaspoon Salt
2 1 teaspoon soda
  1 cup Shortening
1½ cups sugar
3 eggs, well beaten
1 package None Such Mince Meat

Sift flour, salt & soda
Cream shortening, add sugar gradually
Add eggs, beat until smooth.
Add mince meat broken in small
pieces. Add flour & mix well.
Drop by teaspoonfuls on greased
baking sheet. Bake in oven 400° - 12 min.

Molasses Popcorn Balls

3/4 cup water
1 1/2 .. molasses
1 1/2 .. light brown sugar
1 T. vinegar
1/4 teasp. baking soda
1/8 .. cream tarter
3/4 cup butter
1 teasp. vanilla   18-24 balls
3 qts popcorn

Mix first six ingredients in large
sauce pan, place over low
heat and stir until sugar is
dissolved. Bring to boiling
and cook slowly until it will
form a soft ball. Add butter
and cook until hard ball stage
add vanilla & corn form into ball

Molasses Popcorn Balls

¾ cup water

1 ½ cups molasses

1 ½ cups light brown sugar

1 tablespoon vinegar

¼ teaspoon baking soda

⅛ teaspoon cream of tartar

¾ cup butter

1 teaspoon vanilla

3 quarts popcorn

Mix first six ingredients in large saucepan. Place over low heat and stir until sugar is dissolved. Bring to boiling and cook slowly until it will form a soft ball. Add butter and cook until hard ball stage. Add vanilla and corn. Form into balls.

Makes 18 to 24 balls.

Found in *New Magic in the Kitchen* (no author). Published by Borden (no date; circa 1940s?).

DATE TORTE COOKIES

❧

2 eggs
1 cup confectioner's sugar
2 tablespoons flour
½ teaspoon salt
1 teaspoon baking powder
1 cup pitted dates, cut up
1 cup chopped nuts

Beat eggs until fluffy. Add sugar, beating until thick. Sift dry ingredients together. Mix dates and nuts into flour mixture. Fold in egg mixture.

Spread in a greased 9-by-9-by-2-inch pan. Bake at 350 for 30 to 35 minutes. Cool and cut into squares. Roll in confectioner's sugar.

Found in *Ginny Gordon and the Missing Heirloom* by Julie Campbell. Published by Whitman Publishing Co., 1954.

Date Taste Cookies
2 eggs   350°   16 - 2⅛" sq.
1 cup conf sugar
2 tbl flour
¼ teas salt
⅛ / 1 teas B. powder
1 c. pitted dates cut up
1 C chopped nuts.

Beat eggs till fluffy. add sugar
Beating till thick. Sift dry.
Mix in dates & nuts in flour.
Fold in egg mixture. Spread
in greased 9 × 9 × 2 pan. Bake
350° - 30 - 35 min. Cool & cut
in 16 squares. Roll in conf. sugar.

Praline Wafers.

2 eggs   1 tsp. Vanilla
1/3 cup gran. sugar   3/4 cup flour
1/3 cup lt. brown sugar   1/2 tsp salt
1/3 cup dark corn syrup   6 ozs. pecan halves

Cover cookie sheets with foil.
Beat eggs add sugars Beat in
corn syrup & vanilla. Add flour & salt.
Drop level tablespoons of batter
several inches apart, no more
than 9 to a sheet. Top with nuts.
Bake in oven 375° – 10 min or Browned
Note! Use fresh foil for each
batch of cookies.

Praline Wafers

2 eggs
1 teaspoon vanilla
⅓ cup granulated sugar
¾ cup flour
⅛ teaspoon salt
½ cup light brown sugar
6 ounces pecan halves
½ cup dark corn syrup

Cover cookie sheets with foil.

Beat eggs. Add sugar. Beat in corn syrup and vanilla. Add flour and salt.

Drop level tablespoonfuls of batter several inches apart, no more than 9 to a sheet. Top with nuts.

Bake in oven, 375 degrees, 10 minutes or until browned.

Note: Use fresh foil for each batch of cookies.

Found in *New Orleans Recipes* by Mary Moore Bremer. Published by Dorothea Thompson, 1953.

SPRINGERLE

4 eggs
2 cups sugar
4 drops anise oil
4½ cups sifted cake flour

Beat eggs until thick. Gradually add sugar, beating well after each addition. When all sugar has been added, beat for 15 minutes on electric mixer, or 30 minutes by hand.

Blend in anise oil. Lightly fold in cake flour. Dough will be quite stiff.

Roll out to ¼ inch thick on a lightly floured board. Flour springerle pin and roll firmly over dough. Cut cookies along the imprinted edges. Place on buttered cookie sheet. Let dry overnight in cool place.

Bake in 300 degree oven for 30 minutes. Store a month in a covered jar with an orange or an apple. Makes 3 dozen.

Found in *The Sherlock Holmes Cookbook*
by Sean Wright and John Farrell.
Published by Bramhall House, 1976.

Springerle (Use big bowl)

- Beat until thick 4 eggs
- Add gradually 2 c. sugar
- Beat well after each addition. When all sugar has been added, beat 15 minutes on electric mixer or 30 minutes by hand.
- Blend in 4 drops anise oil
- Fold in lightly 4½ c. sifted cake flour
- Dough will be quite stiff. Roll ¼" thick on lightly floured board. (Use ordinary rolling pin.)
- Flour the springerle pin and roll firmly over the dough.
- Cut cookies along the imprinted edges.
- Place on buttered cookie sheet.
- Let dry over night in cool place.
- Bake in 300° oven, 30 minutes.
- Store a month in covered jar with an orange or apple. Makes 3 dozen.

Found in *The Wartime Cook Book* by Alice Bradley. Published by the World Publishing Co., 1943.

Serve upside down with whipped cream. Serves 8 to 10.

Dutch Apple Cake

2 cups sifted flour
3 teaspoons baking powder
2 tablespoons sugar
½ teaspoon salt
¼ cup Spry
1 egg, well beaten
¾ cup milk
3 tablespoons Spry
1 tablespoon butter
¾ cup brown sugar, firmly packed
1 teaspoon cinnamon
1 tablespoon top milk
2 cups apples, sliced.

Sift flour with baking powder, sugar + salt. Cut in ¼ cup Spry until mixture is as fine as corn meal. Combine beaten egg + milk + add to flour mixture, mixing until a soft dough is formed. Melt 3 tablespoons Spry + butter together; add brown sugar, cinnamon, + milk, & mix well. Pour into 8 x 8 inch pan greased with Spry. Press apple slices into mixture in circles. Spread dough over apples. Bake in moderate oven (350°F.) 50 to 60 min.

Dutch Apple Cake

2 cups sifted flour
3 teaspoons baking powder
2 tablespoons sugar
½ teaspoon salt
¼ cup plus 3 tablespoons Spry (shortening)
1 egg, well beaten
¾ cup plus 1 tablespoon milk
1 tablespoon butter
¾ cup brown sugar, firmly packed
1 teaspoon cinnamon
2 cups apples, sliced

Sift flour with baking powder, sugar, and salt. Cut in ¼ cup shortening until mixture is as fine as corn meal.

Combine beaten egg and ¾ cup milk; add to flour mixture, mixing until a soft dough is formed. Melt 3 tablespoons Spry and butter together; add brown sugar, cinnamon and 1 tablespoon milk, and mix well.

Pour into an 8-by-8-inch pan, greased with shortening. Press apple slices into mixture in circles. Spread dough over apples. Bake in moderate oven (350 degrees) for 50 to 60 minutes.

Serve upside-down with whipped cream. Serves 8 to 10.

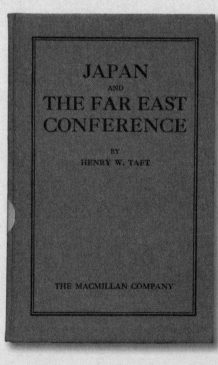

Found in *Japan and the Far East Conference* by Henry W. Taft. Published by the Macmillan Co., 1921.

Jewish Apple Cake

4 lge. Apples)
5 tbspn. Sugar) let stand
3 tspn. Cinnamon)

3 cup Flour)
3 tspn. Baking Powder) sift together
1/2 tspn. Salt)

4 Eggs
1 cup Oil
2 1/2 cups sugar

2½ tspn Vanilla
1/4 cup Orange Juice

1. Peal & slice Apples add Sugar & Cinnamon.

2. Make batter, add dry sifted ingredients.
   Mix well with wooden spoon.

3. Grease Tube Pan.
   Arrange batter and apples in layers,
   ending with batter.

4. Bake for 1¼ hr. until knife comes out clean.
   350o oven.

Note:- Cake tastes better after 2 days.

Applesauce Cake

2½ cups all purpose flour or cake flour
2 cups sugar
1½ tsp soda
1½ tsp salt
¼ tsp baking powder
¾ tsp cinnamon
½ tsp cloves
½ tsp allspice
1½ cups applesauce
½ cup water
½ cup shortening
2 eggs
1 cup raisins
½ cup finely chopped nuts (walnuts)

Heat oven to 350 degrees F.
Grease and flour tube pan.
Measure all ingredients into large mixer bowl.
Blend ½ minute on low speed.
Beat 3 minutes on high speed.
Pour into tube pan.
Bake about 60 minutes or a little longer.
"This makes a very good cake"
                    Mrs. Willie Brown
                    Elkwood, Va.

Found in *Le Creuset Cookbook* by Irena Chalmers.
Published by Potpourri Press, 1980.

APPLESAUCE CAKE

❧

2½ cups all-purpose or cake flour

2 cups sugar

1½ teaspoons baking soda

1½ teaspoons salt

¼ teaspoon baking powder

¾ teaspoon cinnamon

½ teaspoon cloves

½ teaspoon allspice

1½ cups canned applesauce

½ cup water

½ cup shortening

2 eggs

1 cup raisins

½ cup finely chopped walnuts or other nuts

Heat oven to 350 degrees.

Grease and flour a tube pan.

Measure all ingredients into a large mixer bowl. Blend for 30 seconds on low speed. Beat for 3 minutes on high speed.

Pour batter into tube pan. Bake for about 60 minutes or a little longer. This makes a very good cake.

Mrs. Willie Brown, Elkwood, Va.

PRALINE APPLESAUCE CAKE

❧

2¾ cups flour

1⅓ cups sugar

1½ teaspoons baking soda

¼ teaspoon baking powder

1½ teaspoons cinnamon

½ teaspoon cloves

½ teaspoon salt

½ cup shortening

1 can or jar applesauce (1¾ cups)

2 eggs

1½ cups seedless raisins

Grease and flour pan. Sift first seven ingredients together.

Add shortening, applesauce and eggs, then fold in raisins. Pour in pan and bake 35 minutes in oven, 350 degrees.

Cool 15 minutes. Raise oven temperature to broil.

Spread topping (recipe follows) over warm cake and broil 6 inches from heat, 3 to 4 minutes, until topping bubbles up and turns golden. Cool, then cut in squares. Sift confectioner's sugar over cake and wrap in waxed paper.

PRALINE TOPPING

1 stick margarine

¾ cup brown sugar

¼ cup cream

1½ cups chopped pecans

⅔ cup flaked coconut

Cream margarine and brown sugar together. Beat in cream. Stir in pecans and coconut.

Praline Applesauce Cake.

Bake 350° – 55 min (13 x 9 in)

2 3/4 cups flour
1 1/3 " sugar
1 1/2 teas Baking Soda
1/4 teas Baking powder
1 1/2 teas cinnamon
1/2 teas cloves
1/2 teas Salt
1/2 cup shortening
... or for applesauce (1 3/4 cup)
2 eggs   1 1/2 cups raisins

grease + flour pan. Sift 1–7 together
Add shortening + applesauce, eggs then fold in
raisins. Pour in pan + bake 55 min in oven 350°.
Cool 15 min. Raise oven temp. to broil (once)

Praline topping.

1 stick margarine
3/4 cup Brown Sugar
Beat in 1/4 cup cream
Stir in 1 1/2 cups chopped pecans
2/3 cup flaked coconut.

Spread evenly over warm cake + broil 6 inches
from heat. 3 to 4 min until topping bubbles up
and turns golden. Cool then cut in squares
wax paper (11 x 7 cloaf sugar)

Jeanine Larmoth
MURDER ON THE MENU
With Recipes by
Charlotte Turgeon

Food and Drink in the English Mystery Novel

Found in *Murder on the Menu* by
Jeanine Larmoth. Published by
Charles Scribner's Sons, 1972.

¾ lb. shortning - 3 eggs
1 lb. brown sugar - ½ pt molasses
2 cups coffee in this 1 teaspoon
                        soda -
1 lb. raisins - 1 lb. currants -
¼ " citron - lemon - orange peel
1 lb. nuts 2 teaspoons each
of all kinds spices -
extracts the kinds you like
best - little salt
    6 cups flour 3 teaspoons B Poud
use 5 cups first and try out
    this is a large rull I often
cut it down do not bake fast
        I use 2 or 3 kinds
            extracts

        Fruit Cake

Found in *The Boston Cooking-School Cook
Book* by Fannie Merritt Farmer. Published
by Little, Brown and Co., 1928

FRUIT CAKE

❧

¾ pound shortening

3 eggs

1 pound brown sugar

½ pint molasses

2 cups coffee

1 teaspoon baking soda

1 pound raisins

1 pound currants

¼ pound citron, lemon and orange peel

1 pound nuts

2 teaspoons each of all kinds spices, extracts (the ones you like best)

little salt

6 cups flour

3 teaspoons baking powder

Use 5 cups (flour) first and try out. This is a large rule I often cut it down. Do not bake fast. I use 2 or 3 kinds of extracts.

Boston Prune Cake

❧

1 package vanilla pudding mix
1 teaspoon cinnamon
½ teaspoon nutmeg
⅛ teaspoon allspice
1¾ cups milk
⅔ cups chopped prunes
confectioner's sugar

Combine spices and add to pudding mix. Cook pudding as directed. Add chopped prunes and cool.

Spread cooled pudding on a baked yellow cake layer. Add second layer; sprinkle top with confectioner's sugar.

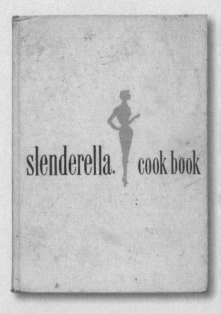

Found in *Slenderella Cook Book*
by Myra Waldo. Published by G. P.
Putnam's Sons, 1957.

Boston Prune Cake

1 pkg Vanilla pudding mix
Combine 1 tsp cinnamon
½ tsp nutmeg + ⅛ tsp Allspice
1 ¾ cups Milk Cook as directed

Add ⅔ cups chopped prunes.
Cool.

Spread cooled mixture on one
of baked yellow cake layers;
Add second layer + sprinkle top
with conf. sugar.

Butterscratch Yule Log.
1 - 6 oz pkg. Butterscotch
          Morsels (1 cup)
1/3 c. sweetened condensed
              milk
1/2 tsp vanilla
1/3 c pecans chopped
Slightly beaten egg white
    Pecan halves.
   Melt over hot (not boiling)
water. Remove from water
Stir in milk & vanilla add
chopped pecans; mix well
Chill until firm to handle.
   Form in 11 in roll on

waxed paper & roll tightly
in waxed paper to shape
evenly. Unroll & mark
surface lengthwise with
tines of fork, brush with
egg white. Press pecan
halves into roll to cover
surface. Wrap in waxed
paper. Chill. Cut in 1/4"
slices with sharp knife.

Butterscotch Yule Log

❧

1 (6-ounce) package butterscotch morsels (1 cup)
⅓ cup sweetened condensed milk
½ teaspoon vanilla
⅓ cup pecans, chopped
slightly beaten egg white
pecan halves

Melt (butterscotch morsels) over hot, not boiling, water. Remove from water. Stir in milk and vanilla. Add chopped pecans; mix well. Chill until firm to handle. Form in ½-inch roll on waxed paper and roll tightly in waxed paper to shape evenly.

Unroll and mark surface lengthwise with tines of fork. Brush with egg white. Press pecan halves into roll to cover surface.

Wrap in waxed paper. Chill. Cut in ½ inch slices with sharp knife.

Found in *The Penguin Cookery Book* by Bee Nilson. Published by Penguin Books, 1952.

CHOCOLATE PORCUPINE

~

4 eggs
⅛ cup sugar
⅛ cup flour
1 teaspoon baking powder
¼ teaspoon salt
½ teaspoon vanilla
chocolate filling and frosting
shredded almonds

Beat eggs until light. Add sugar gradually; continue to beat until thick and smooth.

Sift flour once. Measure and sift with baking powder and salt. Fold into egg mixture. Add vanilla. Turn into a shallow, 10- to 16-inch pan lined with greased paper. Bake in hot oven, 12 to 15 minutes. Remove from oven.

(ends here)

Found in *Flotill Party Book* (no author). Published by Flotill Products International, 1940.

Chocolate Porcupine

4 eggs
7/8 cup sugar
7/8 cup flour
1 t. B. powder
1/4 t. salt
1/2 t. vanilla
Chocolate filling + frosting
shredded almonds.

Beat eggs until light
add sugar gradually continue
to beat until thick & smooth.
Sift flour or a measure
and sift with baking powder
+ salt, fold into egg mixture
add vanilla turn into a
shallow pan 10-14 in. lined with
greased paper. Bake in hot oven
12-15 min. Remove from oven

English Plum pudding.

1 lb. chopped apples let stand 2 days
1 " raisins - 1 lb. currants & lemon peel
½ " citron ~~peel~~. ¾ beef suet 3# B sugar
1 " toasted bread. 1 lb. flour 8 eggs.
2 tbs cinnamon. nutmeg - salt
chop all very fine. put in small
muslin bags. boil 10 hr. serve with
any good sauce -
            this is a tried rule.
        Mrs. Everill, Waterloo N.Y.
P.S. Old english pour a little
brandy on top and light it
just before it is served at
the table, but care must
be taken in doing this -

ENGLISH PLUM PUDDING

~

1 pound chopped apples (let stand 2 days)
1 pound raisins
1 pound currants
¼ lemon peel
½ pound citron
¾ beef suet
3 pounds brown sugar
1 pound toasted bread
1 pound flour
3 eggs
2 tablespoons cinnamon, nutmeg and salt.

Chop all very fine. Put in small muslin bags. Boil 1 hour. Serve with any good sauce.

This is a tried rule.

Mrs. Everill, Waterloo, N.Y.
P.S. Old English pour a little brandy on top and light it just before it is served at the table. But care must be taken in doing this.

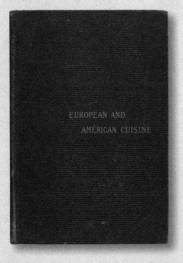

Found in *European and American Cuisine* by Gesine Lemcke. Published by D. Appleton and Co., 1903.

Orange Kiss-me Cake

grind together - 1 large orange, pulp &
rind (reserve juice for topping) - 1 cup
raisins, 1/3 cup walnuts
sift together 2 cups sifted flour, 1 tsp. soda,
1 tsp. salt, 1 cup sugar.
add 1/2 cup shortening, 3/4 cups milk.
Beat - for 2 mins, 300 strokes until batter
is well blended. Elec. mixer blend low speed
then med. speed 2 mins.
add - 2 eggs, unbeaten, 1/4 cup milk, Beat
two mins, fold orange mixture into batter.
Pour - into well greased & lightly floured
12 x 8 x 2 or 13 x 9 x 2 - inch pan. Bake at 350
40 to 50 mins.
Drip 1/3 cup orange juice over warm cake.
Combine 1/3 cup sugar, 1 tsp. cinnamon & 1/3 c
walnuts, sprinkle over cake - Decorate with
orange slices.

Found in *The Modern Hostess Cook Book for This Season, vol. 1, no. 2* by Marjorie Deen. Published by Dell Publishing Co., 1939.

The Modern Hostess
COOK BOOK
for this Season
10¢ NO. 2

Hundreds of Tested Recipes — Interesting Menus
for
Your Budget, Party and Everyday Winter Meals

Orange Kiss-Me Cake

∾

1 large orange, plus another for garnish
1 cup raisins
⅓ cup plus ¼ cup walnuts
2 cups sifted flour
1 teaspoon baking soda
1 teaspoon salt
1 ⅓ cup sugar, divided
½ cup shortening
1 cup milk, divided
2 eggs
⅓ cup orange juice
1 teaspoon cinnamon

Grind orange, including rind, reserving juice. Grind together with raisins and ⅓ cup walnuts.

Sift together flour, baking soda, salt, and 1 cup sugar. Add shortening, ¾ cup milk; beat for 2 minutes or 300 strokes, until shortening is well blended.

Add eggs and ¼ cup milk; beat for 2 minutes. Fold orange mixture into batter. Pour into well-greased and lightly floured 12-by-8-by-2-inch or 13-by-9-by-2-inch pan. Bake at 350 degrees, 40 to 50 minutes.

Drip orange juice over warm cake. Combine ⅓ cup sugar with cinnamon and ¼ cup walnuts. Sprinkle over cake. Decorate with orange slices.

I've enlisted the help of Amy and Hillary from *A Tale of 2 Kitchens* (http://ataleof2kitchens.com) with this recipe. First, let them introduce themselves:

A Tale of 2 Kitchens *was born on a chilly evening in November 2011 after a "Grande Piatto Misto Di Salumi & Formaggi" and two bottles of rosé at New York City's Eataly. Every week, co-bloggers Amy Samuel and Hillary Smith pick a different ingredient or theme to highlight—each of them will create a dish based on the week's topic.*

Together and apart Amy and Hillary do their best to use local, sustainable, and most importantly, seasonal ingredients in all of their recipes. They hope that the enjoyment and good eats they get from ataleof2kitchens will translate into delicious entertainment for all who read it. This Orange Kiss-Me Cake recipe was (thankfully!) fairly easy to decipher and came together very quickly and simply— we popped the juiced orange (we used a naval orange, the recipe didn't specify), raisins, and walnuts into the food processor, and after a couple of minutes they were a yummy, orange-scented paste.

Even though we really appreciated the excruciatingly detailed "300 stroke" mixing note, we opted for the electric mixer option of blending the batter. We baked the cake in a 10-inch round springform pan instead of a rectangular one—it was perfectly done after 40 minutes.

The cinnamon-sugar-walnut topping was absolutely divine, and pouring the freshly squeezed orange juice over the top of the warm cake was key.

Orange Kiss-Me Cake is one of those foods that improves after a day or two—it can be enjoyed for dessert or even breakfast. We can say with authority that anyone who whips up something this tasty deserves a kiss.

AMY SAMUEL AND HILLARY SMITH

FUDGE CAKE

❦

3 tablespoons shortening

12 squares chocolate

½ cup water

1 cup sugar

1 cup flour

½ teaspoon salt

½ teaspoon baking powder

1 egg

¼ cup sour milk

½ teaspoon baking soda

1 teaspoon vanilla

Melt shortening and chocolate in top of a double boiler. Add water and sugar; stir until blended. Remove from heat and set aside.

Combine flour, salt, and baking powder. Stir in egg. Add flour mixture to chocolate; mix well.

Dissolve baking soda in sour milk and add to batter. Add vanilla.

Pour into greased 8-by-8-by-2-inch pan. Bake at 350 degrees for 30 to 35 minutes.

Fudge Cake

3 tbs shortening 2 sq Choc. melted in top of double boiler.

Add ½ cup water & 1 cup Sugar
Stir until blended remove from heat & cool.

1 cup flour
½ tsp Salt
1½ tsp Baking powder
½ / egg

Add egg & flour mixture to choc mixture.

Mix well
¼ cup Sour Milk ½ tsp baking soda
Dissolve soda in milk & add to batter.

1 tsp Vanilla
Pour in Greased pan 8 by 8 by 2"
Bake in 350° oven for 30 to 35 min.

Found in *Lost Lady* by Jude Deveraux. Published by Pocket Books, 1985.

Pineapple Chiffon Cake

7 eggs.
1½ cups sugar
½ cup pine-apple juice
2 tablespoons lemon juice
1 1/4 cups flour (all purpose).
1½ teaspoon baking powder
1/4 teaspoon salt

Separate eggs, Beat egg yolks until thick an
lemon color, divide sugar useing 3/4 cups
for yolks. add to yolks and beat a send
time add, Juice, flour sifted with baking
powder, mix well. then beat egg whites
well with the salt added. fold in

remaining sugar 3/4 cups fold the mixture
with egg yolks mixture pour in ungreased
tube pan, Bake at (352)°° 45 to 50 min
when done turn on cookie sheet and
leave to cool. Then frost.

Hazel.

PINEAPPLE CHIFFON CAKE

7 eggs
1 ½ cups sugar
½ cup pineapple juice
2 tablespoons lemon juice
1 ¼ cups all-purpose flour
1 ½ teaspoons baking powder
¼ teaspoon salt

Separate eggs. Beat egg yolks until thick and lemon-colored. Divide sugar, using ¾ cup for yolks. Add to yolks and beat a second time. Add juice, and flour sifted with baking powder; mix well. Then beat egg whites well with the salt added. Fold in remaining sugar (¾ cup). Fold the mixture with egg yolks mixture. Pour in ungreased tube pan. Bake at 352 degrees, 45 to 50 minutes. When done, turn on cookie sheet and leave to cool. Then frost.

Found in *Adventures in Good Cooking (Famous Recipes) and the Art of Carving in the Home* by Duncan Hines. Published by Adventures in Good Eating, 1945.

Shannon Weber blogs about "the food I want to eat and the food I find interesting" at *A Periodic Table* (http://aperiodictableblog.com). Since a lot of that food seems to be of the sweet variety, I sent her this simple but intriguing Pineapple Chiffon Cake recipe to try. Here's how it went:

I've heard it said that you either love or hate chiffon cake; I love it. Chiffon cakes are majestic things; they're tall, voluminous confections similar to angel food cake, but happily without that slight stickiness some find off-putting. They are sweet but not overly so, possess a delicate, genuine flavor, and are a pitch-perfect accompaniment to fresh, seasonal fruits.

Pineapple chiffon is one of my favorites; its refreshing tropical nature plays well with most any type of berry. The original recipe resulted in a gorgeously textured cake, but it lacked much pineapple flavor. To correct this, I added in some crushed pineapple and reduced the juice down to its tropical essence. I increased the flour to counterbalance the added moisture and increased the salt to further enhance the pineapple flavor. The result was a perfect pineapple chiffon cake, bursting with flavor, and just what I had in mind.

Even though the original recipe didn't list it (beyond the oh-so-descriptive "then frost"), I enjoy my chiffon cake frosted. I paired this one with a coconut frosting infused with reduced pineapple. The frosting is rich, yet light; it's not stiff like a buttercream, just creamy like a cloud. A generous sprinkle of toasted coconut flakes ties all the flavors together.

For this cake, I suggest toasting your coconut before starting to bake. After the cake is in the oven, make your frosting and allow it to chill in the refrigerator. By the time your cake is completely cooled, everything else will be ready for assembly.

Remember, you'll use your reduced pineapple juice for the cake and for the frosting, so don't discard the leftovers when you make the cake.

Chilling the frosting prior to icing your cake allows it to "reset" itself back to its firmer form. That being said, the optimal way to ice this cake is thickly on top; it gives it a billowy, vintage look. Icing the full cake (down the sides) could, depending on the day, leave you with a frosting avalanche. If you insist on a fully-frosted look, use your favorite buttercream recipe instead.

Incorporation is everything with this cake. You don't want to overmix, especially after the egg white addition. Use a gentle but confident hand, taking care to thoroughly mix everything together so there are no odd bumps or uneven rising in your finished cake.

CAKE
7 eggs, separated

1 ½ cups sugar

2 (15-ounce) cans crushed pineapple, drained with juice reserved

½ cup reduced pineapple juice (see below)

2 tablespoons fresh lemon juice, strained (1–2 lemons, depending on size)

1 ½ cups all-purpose flour

1 ½ teaspoons baking powder

½ teaspoon salt

FROSTING
8 ounces cream cheese, softened

½ cup (1 stick) unsalted butter, at room temperature

¼ cup reduced pineapple juice (from the cake recipe;
you should have about ½ cup left over)

½ cup cream from coconut milk* (regular, not reduced fat)

4 cups confectioners' sugar

⅛ teaspoon salt

*If you refrain from shaking the can, the coconut cream stays separated from the coconut water, which falls to the bottom. Open the can carefully, remove the lid, and scoop the cream out into your measuring cup. One 15-ounce can will be plenty.

TOPPING

2 cups sweetened shredded or flaked coconut

TOAST YOUR COCONUT: Preheat oven to 350 degrees F. Spread coconut evenly on a baking sheet lined with parchment paper, breaking up any clumps with your fingers. Bake for 6–8 minutes, stirring every few minutes, taking care to scoop the outer edges inward. Watch it carefully; once toasted, your coconut will have taken on a variegated color, ranging from pale peach to deep golden brown. Let cool completely before topping your cake.

MAKE YOUR CAKE: Preheat (or keep) your oven to 350 degrees. Grease and flour a tube pan with removable bottom, tapping out any excess.

Drain your pineapple in a colander over a medium bowl, squeezing out any excess juice. Set aside juice and 1 cup of the crushed pineapple. In a small saucepan over medium-low heat, bring the pineapple juice to a simmer. Reduce heat slightly and continue to simmer until reduced to 1 cup, about 30 minutes. Stir occasionally. Your end result will be a thick juice, not sticky or syrupy. Set aside to cool completely.

Whisk together the flour, baking powder, and salt. Set aside. Separate your eggs into two large bowls, and be careful not to mix whites with yolks.

Using an electric mixer, whisk egg yolks until slightly beaten. Add half the sugar (¾ cup) to the yolks and beat until lemon-colored and light, 3–4 minutes. Scrape down the sides. Add lemon juice and the ½ cup reduced pineapple juice, and mix until fully incorporated. Scrape down the sides again. Add the flour mixture in two parts, beating each time until just incorporated. Scrape down the sides once more and beat a few more seconds, until homogenous. Stir in 1 cup drained pineapple.

Using clean, dry beaters (and I can't stress this enough: egg whites will not set up if there's even a trace of grease), beat egg whites until soft peaks form. Add the remaining ¾ cup sugar and beat until shiny, thick, and meringue-like in texture, about 4 minutes.

Carefully tip your egg white mixture into the batter, using a rubber spatula to slide the egg whites into the bowl. Use a spoon to scrape the egg white mixture from the spatula. Don't tap it. Using an up-and-over motion, gently and slowly fold your egg white mixture into your batter, rotating the bowl a little with each fold. This is the most important part of getting a chiffon right; treat it as such and work with patience.

Once your batter is homogenous slide it into your tube pan, gently smoothing the top with your spatula. Place on a center rack in the oven and bake for 45–50 minutes, checking for doneness at the 40-minute mark.

When done, the cake should be a medium golden brown on top and no longer wet, with a cake tester inserted in the center of the batter coming out clean.

MAKE YOUR FROSTING: In a large bowl using an electric mixer, cream your butter and cream cheese until light and fluffy, 2–3 minutes. Scrape down sides. Add the reduced pineapple juice, cream from coconut milk, and salt, and beat until incorporated, about 30 seconds. Scrape down sides again. Begin adding your confectioners' sugar, 1 cup at a time, beating after each addition until incorporated. Your frosting should be creamy and not stiff; this frosting sets up and gets thicker when refrigerated. If you want a thicker frosting, add more confectioners' sugar, ½ cup at a time, until it reaches desired consistency. Chill in the refrigerator for at least 1 hour before frosting your completely cooled cake.

This cake, with the frosting, is best eaten the day it's made. If you leave it unfrosted, the cake will be fine at room temperature, if tightly covered, for up to three days.

SHANNON WEBER

Memorandum

From the Office of

Ralph J. Rivers, M.C.

Simple Pound Cake

1 cup Shortening

1/2 tea. Salt

1 1/2 cups Sugar

1 Tea. Baking Powder

5 eggs

1/2 cup Sweet Milk

2 cups Flour

1 tea. Vanilla

Cream shortening and
sugar together and

egg — one at a time
beating after adding
each egg. add flour,
salt, Baking Powder
sifted, together, and
Sweet milk. Bake
350° for 1 hour.

Simple Pound Cake

1 cup shortening
½ teaspoon salt
1½ cups sugar
1 teaspoon baking powder
5 eggs
½ cup sweet milk
2 cups flour
1 teaspoon vanilla

Cream shortening and sugar together. Add eggs, one at a time, beating after adding each egg. Sift together flour, salt and baking powder, and add to mixture. Add milk and vanilla. Bake at 350 degrees for 1 hour.

Found in *The Co-ed Cookbook* by Henrietta Flack. Published by Scholastic Book Services, 1967.

Butter Scotch Pie.

2 eggs 1 cup B sugar - salt
2 large, tbsp butter, 3 tbsp flour
2½ cups milk use 1 whole egg and
1 yolk, mix well - cook in double
boiler. have a good crust
baked. fill shell and cover
with white of egg beaten.

Green tomato pie.

1 pt. green tomatoes chopped fine
3 good apples. 2 large cups sugar
½ cup molasses ½ cup vinegar
piece of butter spice to taste
little salt, cook 20 min stir
3 tbsp flour wet in a little
water stir all toge. then heat - well
1 large cup raisins. this makes 3
Pies.

Found in *The Modern Cook Book* by K.
Camille Den Dooven. Published by
Basic Books, 1945.

The Modern COOK BOOK

COMPLETE
Essential
Cooking
Lessons for
Beginners.
Economical
Wholesome
Recipes
from Soup
to Nuts.

It is easy to Cook with this book as your Guide

Butter Scotch Pie

❧

2 eggs
1 cup brown sugar
salt
2 large tablespoons butter
3 tablespoons flour
2½ cups milk

Use one whole egg and one yolk, mix well. Cook in double boiler.

Have a good crust baked.

Fill shell and cover with white of egg beaten.

Green Tomato Pie

❧

1 pint green tomatoes, chopped fine
3 good apples
2 large cups sugar
½ cup molasses
½ cup vinegar
piece of butter
spice, to taste
little salt
1 large cup raisins

Cook 20 minutes, stir 3 tablespoons flour wet in a little water. Stir all together, heat well.

This makes 3 pies.

Through the blog, I've been lucky enough to get to know Lyssa Oberkreser, a librarian, photographer, and food blogger from Florida. Her blog, *Mypiary* (http://mypiary.com), is all about the wonderful world of pies. I sent her the recipe for Butter Scotch Pie. Here's what she came up with:

Having spent the last year researching pie recipes, I learned that most were made with ingredients on hand. Fresh fruit was used when in season, and cream pies filled the gap between crops. Cream pies are usually made with milk, butter, sugar, and egg yolks, saving the egg whites for a festive meringue. Brown sugar, rather than granulated sugar, gives this pie its delightful butterscotch flavor.

This found recipe called for 1 whole egg and 1 egg yolk, which is quite frugal considering most cream pie recipes call for at least 3 or 4 egg yolks. Using a double-boiler was another unique twist to this recipe, which I liked because it kept the filling from scorching or cooking too quickly.

Afraid that my pie would come out a little skimpy, I chose to use 4 egg yolks, using the whites for a fluffy meringue. Flour or cornstarch can be used as a thickener, but I prefer cornstarch for a smoother texture. I also used dark brown sugar for richer flavor and added 1 teaspoon of vanilla extract. The hot filling should be poured into a cooled, pre-baked piecrust, topped with meringue, and baked for about 12–15 minutes in a 350-degree oven.

This pie was declared "Outstanding!" by my official pie taster.

LYSSA OBERKRESER

CARAMEL CUSTARD PIE

❧

6 tablespoons sugar
2 cups milk
3 eggs
½ teaspoon vanilla
⅛ teaspoon salt
pastry

Melt and brown sugar. Add milk and stir until sugar dissolves. Beat eggs. Pour milk mixture on them and add vanilla and salt. Turn into pie tin lined with pastry. Bake for 40 minutes.

CUSTARD SAUCE

2 cups milk
⅓ cup sugar
pinch of salt
1 tablespoon cornstarch
2 egg yolks or 1 egg, beaten
½ teaspoon vanilla

Heat milk. Add sugar, salt, and cornstarch, and stir until thick. Cook 15 minutes. Add egg and cook for a few minutes longer, stirring all the time. Cool and add vanilla.

ustard Sauce
cups milk
cup sugar
inch salt
ttl cornstarch
egg ylks or whole egg
teas vanilla.

eat milk, add sugar etc.
stir until thick. Cook 15 min
Add beaten egg & cook
few min. longer. Stir all time
cool & add vanilla.

Carmel Custard Pie
6 ttl sugar
2 cups milk
3 eggs
½ teas vanilla
⅛ teas. salt

Pastry
Melt & brown sugar
Add milk & stir till
sugar dissolved. Beat
eggs pour milk mixture
over them & add sugar salt
vanilla. Pour into lined with
pastry and bake 40 min

1 can tomato soup
1 onion (sml)
2 tbsp. catsup
½ lt Am cheese
tooster crackers.

Found in *Food for Lovers* by
Almuth Elgeti. Published by
MacFadden, 1963.

Fresh Fruit Ice Cream Pie

Baked Pie shell.
   Make meringue of 4 egg
whites & sugar.
   Use any fruit inside, cover
with meringue on top & brown!

   Vanilla or other ice cream
2 c. apple sauce in shell (canned)
Spread ice cream on top of sauce.
Spread meringue on top. &
put in oven. 3 or 4 min.
& serve immediately.

Fresh Fruit Ice Cream Pie

4 egg whites
sugar
2 cups fruit or applesauce
vanilla or other ice cream
baked piecrust

Make meringue of egg whites and sugar.

Use any fruit inside piecrust. Spread ice cream over fruit. Spread meringue on top and put in oven for 3 or 4 minutes to brown. Serve immediately.

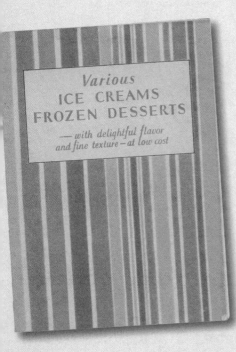

Found in *Various Ice Creams Frozen Desserts* (no author). Published by Pet Milk Co., 1928.

PRUNE MERINGUE PIE

1½ cups cooked prunes, cut up
1 cup liquid from prunes
1 cup crushed pineapple
¼ cup granulated sugar
3 tablespoons cornstarch
¼ teaspoon salt
3 eggs
1 pie shell

Combine prunes, liquid, and pineapple over heat. Blend sugar, cornstarch, and salt. Stir into hot fruit. Cook until mixture is clear.

Beat egg yolks. Stir a little hot fruit mixture into egg. Stir egg slowly into remaining fruit. Cook for 3 or 4 minutes longer over low heat.

Pour into pie shell. Put meringue on top and brown in oven, 325 degrees, for 15 to 20 minutes.

Easy recipes for delicious meals at low cost by the master chef who by radio and books has taught hundreds of thousands his practical skill.

THE MYSTERY CHEF'S *never fail* COOK BOOK

Found in *The Mystery Chef's Never Fail Cook Book* (no author). Published by Perma Giants, 1949.

Prune Meringue Pie.

1 1/2 cups cooked prunes (cut up)
1 cup liquid from prunes.
1 " crushed pineapple
1/4 " Granulated sugar
3 tablespoons cornstarch
1/4 teas. salt
3 eggs
1 pie shell.

Combine cut up prunes, liquid, pineapple
+ heat. Blend sugar, cornstarch + salt
+ stir in hot fruit. Cook until mixture
is clear. Beat egg yolks + add stir
a little hot fruit in + stir slowly
into remaining fruit. Cook 3 or 4 min.
longer over low heat. Put meringue
on top and brown in oven 325°
for 15 - 20 min.

Apricot Bavarian Cream

3½ t. gelatine

5 T. cold water

¾ C. evaporated milk

½ C. sugar

1 C. apricot juice

⅛ t. salt

1 egg white

1½ C. apricot pulp.

Soak ½ t. gelatine in 1 T. water 5 min. Scald milk in double boiler add gelatine and stir. Chill. Soak rest of gelatine in water dissolve over hot water add sugar salt and apricot juice, when mixture begins to thicken fold in beaten egg white and pulp. Whip the cold milk until stiff and fold into fruit mixture. Chill until firm.

FRANK EDWARDS

Author of "Stranger Than Science" Presents

STRANGE PEOPLE

A COLLECTION OF TRUE STORIES ABOUT

continued on front flap

Found in *Strange People* by Frank Edwards
Published by Lyle Stuart, 1961.

APRICOT BAVARIAN CREAM

✑

3½ teaspoons gelatin

5 tablespoons cold water

¾ cups evaporated milk

½ cup sugar

1 cup apricot juice

⅛ teaspoon salt

1 egg white

1½ cups apricot pulp

Soak ½ teaspoon gelatin in 1 tablespoon water for 5 minutes. Scald milk in double boiler. Add gelatin and stir. Chill.

Soak rest of gelatin in water. Dissolve over hot water. Add sugar, salt, and apricot juice. When mixture begins to thicken, fold in beaten egg white and pulp. Whip the cold milk until stiff, and fold into fruit mixture. Chill until firm.

Rice Dainty

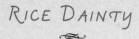

¾ cup cooked rice
¾ cup fruit, chopped up
½ cup honey
¾ cup cream, whipped

Mix rice, fruit, and honey. Fold in whipped cream and chill well.

Found in *Sixty-Five Delicious Dishes Made with Bread* by Marino Harris Neil. Published by the Fleischmann Co., 1919.

Rice Dainty

(Pudding)

3/4 c. cooked rice
3/4 c. fruit-chopped up
1/2 c honey
3/4 c. cream -whipped

Mix rice, fruit + honey.
Fold in whipped cream
+ chill well.

I sent this recipe to Cara Reed, the blogger behind *Fork and Beans* (www.forkandbeans.wordpress.com). The site specializes in gluten-free and allergy-free creations, refusing to use the words "I can no longer eat that!" Cara strives to transform all of your favorite classics (Cheez-Its, Girl Scout cookies, doughnuts) into something not only edible but comparable to what you remembered them tasting like, all without the gluten, eggs, and dairy. She explains:

> *Rice Dainty is a guaranteed crowd-pleaser for all rice pudding lovers! The honey in this recipe lightly sweetens the rice and the richness of the cream balances out all of the flavors, bringing you the perfect quick-fix dessert. Simply add some chopped almonds (optional) for texture and top with a dollop of whipped cream, and you will be in heaven—if heaven is sweet, creamy, and full of rice.*
>
> *For a nondairy option, use MimiCreme unsweetened "cream" in place of the whipping cream.*

CARA REED

Peach Smoothee

1 can (2 cups) Peach Pie Filling
1 15oz. can condensed milk
1 tbsp lemon juice
1/2 cup chopped pecans
2 tbsp. chopped candied ginger
1 1/2 cup whipping cream,
                    whipped.

Beat pie filling + milk until peaches are crushed. Mix in lemon juice, pecans + candied ginger. Fold in cream. Pour in 3 ice-cube trays + freeze until firm. Makes 1 1/2 qts.

PEACH SMOOTHEE

1 can (2 cups) peach pie filling
1 (15-ounce) can condensed milk
1 tablespoon lemon juice
½ cup chopped pecans
2 tablespoons candied ginger
1½ cups whipping cream, whipped

Beat pie filling and milk until peaches are crushed. Mix in lemon juice, pecan, and candied ginger. Fold in cream. Pour in 3 ice-cube trays and freeze until firm. Makes 1½ quarts.

Found in *Slenderella Cook Book*
by Myra Waldo. Published by
G. P. Putnam's Sons, 1957.

Coconut Dreams

꩜

BOTTOM LAYER
2 cups sifted flour
¼ cup sugar
1 teaspoon salt
1 cup soft butter

TOP LAYER
2 eggs
1 teaspoon vanilla
1 ½ cup light brown sugar
2 tablespoons flour
¼ teaspoon salt
½ teaspoon baking powder
½ cup shredded coconut
1 cup coarsely chopped walnuts

Combine 2 cups flour, ¼ cup sugar, 1 teaspoon salt, add butter, and mix until smooth. Spread on bottom of oblong baking dish. Bake 350 degrees for 10 minutes, firm but not brown. Remove from oven.

While bottom layer is baking, beat 2 eggs until fluffy, mix brown sugar, vanilla, 2 tablespoons flour, ½ teaspoon salt, ½ teaspoon baking powder. Beat until smooth. Stir in coconut and nuts. Spread over bottom layer. Bake 350 degrees for 20 minutes.

coconut dreams

2 c. sifted flour
¼ c. sugar
1 tsp. salt
1 c. soft butter
} Bottom Layer

2 eggs
1 tsp. vanilla
1-½ c. lt. brown sugar
2 tblsp. flour
¼ tsp. salt
} Top Layer
½ tsp. bak. powder
½ c. shredded coco-nut
1 c. coarsely chopped walnuts

(over)

Combine 2 c. flour, ¼ c. sugar, 1 tsp. salt, add butter and mix until smooth. Spread on bottom of an oblong baking dish. Bake 350° for 10 mins., firm but not brown. Remove from oven. While bottom layer is baking, beat 2 eggs until fluffy, mix brown sugar, vanilla, 2 tblsp. flour + ½ tsp. salt + b. powder. Beat until smooth. Stir in coconut + nuts. Spread over bottom layer. Bake 350° for 20 mins.
7" × 11"

Found in *Social Etiquette of New York*.
Published by D. Appleton and Co., 1885.

Thanks

The biggest helping of thanks goes to my wife, who helped sort through, decipher and edit these recipes. This is her book as much as mine.

I would also like to thank my recipe testers, who were able to deliver great work on a tight schedule. I hope the readers of this book go on to discover and enjoy their websites as much as I have.

Finally, I would like to thank my agent Kate McKean and editor Maria Gagliano, as well as the editors and designers behind the scenes. Despite my best efforts, they always make me look good.

About the Author

MICHAEL POPEK studied literature at Bennington College before rejoining his family's used-book business. He lives and works in Oneonta, New York, with his wife, his daughter, two dogs, and a cat.